PERTEMPS TO DREAM

Isobel Coltman has ridden horses at the Real Escuela Andaluza del Arte Ecuestre in Jerez, played cello at the Royal Albert Hall and been stranded on a Greek island, escaping on a small fishing boat in the middle of the night.

Isobel comes from London, where she kept her pony, Misty, in the back garden. Misty accompanied her owner to York University, but only Isobel got a Degree in Language and Linguistic Science.

A keen cello player from an early age, and a member of two orchestras, Isobel's passion has always been horses and Misty was joined by a beautiful chestnut mare, Ara.

Moving to Gloucestershire with Ara and Misty, Isobel met her future husband, Gary. They bred a family of successful racehorses as well as a son of their own.

Isobel now lives in Malvern with son Ross. The Aramis family live together in a field nearby.

"I am grateful for the contributions of my parents, Barbara and Derek, whose memories have added to this incredible story."

PERTEMPS TO DREAM
FROM COWSHED TO CHELTENHAM

ISOBEL COLTMAN

WITH
BARBARA COLTMAN
DEREK COLTMAN

ARAMIS

In loving memory of my husband, Gary

Contents

Foreword

Our future champion was born on 27th April, 2002. Isobel's family name is Coltman. Her ancestors, presumably, looked after horses. Isobel married Gary Phipps. Phipps comes from the Greek "philhippos', meaning someone who likes horses. This combination, you might agree, sounds like a propitious beginning for a bay colt. To add icing to the cake, Kayf Aramis was born in the Chinese Year of the Horse!

Isobel and Gary's son was born four months later, on 3rd August. He was given the name, Ross. This is not only a good Scottish name but, as German philologists will tell you, it is an old High German word for a knight's steed. The word 'Ross', in fact, came into the English language via a strange process called metathesis (consonant and vowel switching places) and ended up as 'orse'. Later it acquired the 'h' which makes it sound much more respectable and noble. Interestingly enough, the well-known ex-jockey and racing commentator, John Francome, seems well aware of the linguistic origins and still keeps the original pronunciation – 'orse'! Unless he has an aversion to 'aitches'!!

Anyway, I digress. This new colt's Sire is the famous Kayf Tara, the champion two-miler, stayer, who won the Ascot Gold Cup twice, the Irish St. Leger twice, the Yorkshire Cup, the Goodwood Cup. What a hard act to follow!! His Dam is Ara. She didn't race but has a racing pedigree. The birth was a combination of other coincidences. Isobel was very keen on show-jumping and dressage – you know, the sport that some people ' up North' describe as 'like watching paint dry'! She had arranged to send her pedigree mare to Somerset to be 'covered' – hate that word! - by an eventing stallion. As luck or not would have it there was an outburst of foot and mouth disease and Isobel was unable to travel outside the county of Gloucestershire. But that did not stop her for long. She discovered that there was a stud farm not far away called Overbury, where, as chance would have it, Kayf Tara was 'standing' (another strange word!). It was this stallion's first year at Overbury. After eight major wins from ten races he had injured himself in Australia and had to retire from racing. So that was it. The plot was hatched.

Oh. By the way, this colt's name is Aramis – Kayf Aramis. (That sounds like how James Bond introduces himself!) Rather a nice sounding name, don't you think? How did he get it? No. Nothing to do with Aramis perfume, though it is tempting to jump to that conclusion. Later, an attempt was made to persuade the Company that makes the famous perfume to become a sponsor but the managing director turned out to be a golf fanatic and had no interest whatsoever in horse racing. Not named after one of the Three Musketeers either! No his is a clever combination created by his owner. Quite a good name, don't you think? You'll find out how it came about later.

As the subtitle of this book suggests, Kayf Aramis was not born in lavish surroundings despite his aristocratic-sounding name. Neither is his owner from one of those wealthy horse-owning families. She just dreamt of owning a race horse, well originally a dressage horse, even if she did not have much money. Everything seemed to work out for her. She was lucky that the local farmer had an old, at that time, disused cowshed, which he very generously allowed to be used as the place of birth. Sounds almost biblical, doesn't it? 'Born in a stable because there was no room at the inn!!' For 'stable' read 'cowshed'! In fact if you look at the picture opposite you will see that this metaphor is not so misplaced. There's no ass standing by but there's a pony!

Derek Coltman

Kayf Aramis

Isobel, the farmer and his family regard the newly born colt

Preface

Join me on a magical ride to the top of the Malvern Hills with Kayf Aramis, as we enjoy glorious Elgar country, quintessential English countryside, and I reminisce on the events which led to my little horse, born in a cowshed rising to winning at the pinnacle of jump racing, the Cheltenham Festival.

Growing up in London seems an unlikely place to develop a lifelong passion for horses and yet it was my childhood dream to have my own pony. This dream miraculously came true with my beautiful grey Welsh/Arab pony Misty who lived in our back garden near Hampstead Heath.

Ara, a stunning chestnut Thoroughbred mare later joined Misty and together we moved to Gloucestershire, where I met my future husband, Gary.

Kayfi's race record in the Racing Post reads 85 races: 7 wins, 16 seconds and 7 thirds and £153,670 in prize money; his rating rising from 45 on the flat to become one of the top hurdlers in the country with a rating of 149.

However, behind these impressive statistics is a small horse with a big personality; a very special horse held in such affection by so many people, in a racing career which spanned ten years, and even had his own fan club.

Aidan Coleman, who rode Kayfi to victory, commented: *"A special horse. Tough and genuine."*

Part One tells the story of how Kayf was born in a cowshed and his big race day, while on a ride to the Malvern Hills.

In Part Two, you will read my Dad's humorous and interesting account of Kayfi's racing career from a family perspective.

I have enjoyed riding Kayfi since he retired from racing, and I am constantly in awe of how much such a little horse achieved on the racetrack and yet is quite content to hack out with me.

When Kayfi left the farm on which he was born to go into training, we had no idea what amazing journeys he was going to take us on and would never have believed he would be returning home a Cheltenham Festival winner!

'**Pertemps to Dream**' is the story of Kayf Aramis, but it is also about the people that helped him along the way and his horse family at home. Kayfi is just one of the family.

In writing this book, I wish to share the story of Kayf Aramis and to thank everyone who has been involved in this very special little horse.

I hope you enjoy Kayfi's tale as much as we do.
Dreams can come true.

Isobel with baby Kayf Aramis

Isobel Coltman
Malvern, 2019

Isobel with racehorse Kayf Aramis

Acknowledgements

Horse breeding and horse racing is harder than I thought and yet more rewarding than I could ever have imagined. None of this would have been possible without Gary and my family, together with all the people at the racing yard.

My late husband, **Gary,** who happily and always with a wicked sense of humour, took on the role of groom in both its meanings. He always supported me in my crazy schemes, paid bills for stud fees (when ringing Simon Sweeting at Overbury Stud to ask for yet another deal on stud fees, Simon said *"Tell her you made me cry"*) and basically put up with me where I'm sure no one else would have done.

When we got married, Gary's Dad told him to get used to eating potatoes. This sounds like a strange piece of marital advice, but came in very handy when the numbers of horses and subsequent costs kept increasing.

Gary was in charge of the camera at races, annoying Becky by taking so many photos of her in the parade ring with Kayfi, until our son Ross was old enough to take over as chief race photographer when the photos became a little more, how shall I say... interesting, with lower camera angles and close-ups.

My son **Ross,** who as a baby had to wait patiently in a pram next to the stable while I took care of Ara and young Kayfi; and later wearing mini jockey silks to the races, until he was old enough to say 'no'!

My Dad has been Daily Racing News Blogger for Aramis Racing since 2013, writing interesting blogs on the lighter side of racing combined with humorous titles. Derek had already written "On the Level" which now forms part two of **Pertemps to Dream** and he has added a chapter on jump racing.

My love of horseracing was born from our weekly Saturday morning jaunts to the local betting shop to put a pound on a horse to win and cheer them home in the afternoon. The kitty rose to over £100, only to dwindle eventually back down to zero.

My Mum who when Kayfi was a very green, naughty and slow two-year-old in training, proclaimed that Kayfi would be a winner one day. She says:

"True Grit, character and absolute belief that the tiny little 'origami' foal would grow up to be a winner. Totally irrational, but he's living proof that dreams can come true."

Not even a triple-heart bypass kept her from cheering Kayfi on to victory at Cheltenham. An eloquent writer, she has contributed the chapters *What's in a Name?* and *How it all Began.*

Auntie Sue and Uncle Bill for their support at the races and the legendary race picnics.

My brothers Dominic and Alexis for all their help and support.
The priceless story of Dominic, who sneaks out of work to watch Kayfi's race and notices that the barbers around the corner have a big TV screen showing the Cheltenham Festival. He goes in for a haircut just so he can watch the race. "That's my sister's horse," he tells the barber. The barber quickly rushes off to put a bet on the race. The result: "No sir, no, no. This haircut is on me!"

John Goodman and family who enjoyed a year with Kayfi.

Members of the Kayf Aramis Racing Club.

Kayfi's trainers and the jockeys and all the stable staff who helped to make this dream come true.

Becky, who looked after Kayfi for nine years in training and put up with, not just having her photo taken at the races, but our frequent visits to the yard. Becky enjoyed a wonderful partnership with Kayfi, starting at John Spearing's yard in Worcestershire, where Becky was working when Kayfi joined as a three year old, and then continued when they met up again at Nigel Twiston-Davies's yard.

Haggis, who looked after Kayfi at Venetia Williams yard with great dedication and good humour. They enjoyed a fantastic year together.

Haggis: "He is a wonderful horse gave me some special moments especially Cheltenham"

"He's also the only horse in the last 10 years that I have fallen off as he spooked at something on the walkway and whipped round and I fell off landing on my feet with him just looking at me as if to say: What you doing? Get back on stupid woman!"

Sponsor **iQ Optical**.

The **Aramis Family.**
Ara and sons and daughters: **Kayf Aramis, Kaylifa Aramis, Kaylif Aramis and Kaylina Aramis;** and her grandsons: **Zayfire Aramis and Berlief Aramis.**
With great sadness I said farewell to Ara this year, at the age of 29.

Isobel with the Aramis family (left to right) Kaylifa, Ara, Bertie, Kaylina, Kayfi

What's in a Name?

A HORSE REGISTERED FOR RACING adheres to the name given it at the debut of its racing career regardless of what it might have been known as by the breeder or by what nickname, benign or otherwise, it acquired in the training yard.

A glance through any race card will show names reflecting a range of emotions, hopes and fears of the owner or the syndicate, from commemorating a person or event in their lives or in history to a gobbledygook, incomprehensible mouthful of syllables to challenge the race commentator.

These highly-bred, noble animals surely deserve respect so why is it that some horses are given silly or pejorative names? Is it perhaps to catch the public's attention when your horse is unlikely to win. At least it has the power to amuse the excited crowd and give you some kudos? Some owners go to great lengths to mystify the committee whose job it is to scrutinise names of horses new to racing and pass, what on paper looks innocent enough, but in pronunciation bring a smile to spectators as the commentators struggle with:-

Ha Ha Ha
AARRRRRRR
Hoof Hearted - Who WHAT!
Passing Wind - What schoolboy humour!
Hucking Hot! – That got past the censor!

A classic was the Aug 22 2010 commentary from the 7th race at Monmouth Park where the commentator had to handle this mouthful:

<u>**My Wife Knows Everything**</u> battled with <u>**The Wife Doesn't Know**</u> to the exciting finish, coming first and second, respectively. Hilarious! The commentator had the crowds roaring with laughter although perhaps not so funny for the husbands who had to face their wives that night!

SO WHAT'S IN A NAME?

As SHAKESPEARE elegantly put it in 'Romeo and Juliet'

"What's in a name? That which we call a rose
By any other name would smell as sweet."

One cannot argue with Shakespeare; he sussed out all human emotions and paraded them in his work. Yet, give the rose a name and the generic rose transforms itself into a magical world of senses to delight the mind and give it a myriad of possibilities, each unique to the individual and his/her experience in life.

Names matter!

Consider the following named rose bushes available in reputable rose growers' collections, which are also names of racehorses:-

King's Ransom

Full of rich golden treasure
"A Horse, a horse, my kingdom for a horse" cries King Richard III

Albertine

The memorable character in Proust's great novel
"A la recherche du temps perdu"

You're Beautiful

You're beautiful, you're beautiful, it's true I saw your face in a crowded place And I don't know what to do 'Cause I'll never be with you, James Blunt

Flower Power

A tribute to the 60's Hippy generation who placed flowers in the barrel of guns following Timothy Leary's invitation to "Turn on. Tune in. Drop out"

scot

Here the Creme de la Creme gather for the world-famous racing and the ladies parade their delicious confectionary of hats for the world to admire

Rambling Rector

No doubt alludes to the insatiable appetite of some good natured Rectors who go beyond the call of duty to pleasure their flock

Agatha Christie

Would surely have created murder and mayhem in the haunted rectories,enveloped in ghostly mists

Mama Mia!

Cries Frankie Dettori, as he performs his famous flying dismount to the delight of his adoring fans. He most memorably rode all seven winners on British Champions' Day at Ascot in 1996

Irish Eyes

Are smiling, and how, at every Cheltenham Festival as, fuelled by a 'drop of the hard stuff' the Irish raiders make off with the moolah......

Sexy Rexi

Scent from Heaven.... if the right conditions prevail, if it is the right track and distance, if the right Jockey on top and if, she feels like running....may, one day have her owners celebrating at the Savoy Hotel.....a big IF.but that's racing folks!

21

So, you still ask, WHAT'S IN A NAME?

The above names of roses, their initials spelling 'Kayf Aramis', give a particular nuance to each bloom. In the same way, Racehorses are given official names which more often than not reflect on their character, or on the wishes or hopes of the owners. Who can forget:-

Frankel, named after the famous American Trainer
Shergar likely based on a Persian word
Desert Orchid after a beautiful flower
Red Rum from his parents Ma**red** and Quo**rum**
Dancing Brave is self explanatory
Nijinski a superb mover
See the Stars as the example of hope.

Shakespeare also gave horses in his plays meaningful names

Barbary in Othello   **Capilet** in Twelfth Night

Surrey in Richard III   **Galathe** in Henry V

He had great love and respect for the animal.
For their Loyalty, Grace and Strength

Oh for a horse with wings!

I will not change my horse with any that treads but on four pasterns. *Ça, ha!* He bounds from the earth as if his entrails were hairs: *le cheval volant*, the **Pegasus**, *qui a les narines de feu!* When I bestride him, I soar, I am a hawk: he trots the air; the earth sings when he touches it; the basest horn of his hoof is more musical than the pipe of Hermes

Henry V

Were these the thoughts of Aidan Coleman as he rode Kayf Aramis to victory when he thundered up the final slope on the 'diminutive' race horse who proved himself on the field of battle in The Pertemps at the Cheltenham Festival in 2009.

IS THERE MAGIC IN THE KAYF ARAMIS NAME?

Beginning at the tail-end, so to speak, the <u>MIS</u> of Aramis is, in fact from **Misty**, a much loved pony, not, as some might think, from the distinctive men's aftershave, nor from the name of one of the Three Musketeers in the novel by Alexandre Dumas**, Athos, Porthos** and **Aramis** whose motto was, as we all know,

"All for One and One for All"

A motto willingly and naturally adopted by the Aramis family, who may bicker among themselves in the field, but, like in the best of families, stand up for each other too.

<u>ARA</u>**,** preceding the **MIS,** is the name of the dam, the horse Isobel found for sale in **Horse and Hound** magazine and persuaded her grandpa to top up the loan she got from the bank. He didn't take much persuading and Grandpa, having ridden horses as a young Officer, willingly entered into collusion with her and the deed was done before her parents returned from a week-end trip to New York.

ARA came from racing stock but had not been raced herself. She is a handsome chestnut mare and gave Isobel fine rides on North London tracks before moving to Gloucestershire where she became the mother of all mothers in bearing not only **Kayf Aramis**, her first foal, but subsequent foals each with good character and prestige for **Aramis Racing**.

Isobel and Ara in North London

Finally <u>KAYF,</u> taking his first name after **Kayf Tara,** the sire who had only recently arrived at the nearby **Overbury Stud** after an illustrious career winning :-

The Gold Cup in 1998 and 2000
The Irish St Leger n 1998 and 1999.
Goodwood Cup, Prix Kergorlay & Prix Vicomptesse Vigier in 1999
The Yorkshire Cup in 2000

And 8-time British National Hunt Sires' Champion

Kayf Tara became the initial spark in the breeding programme of the beautiful family of **Aramis** horses. The team at Overbury, under Simon Sweeting, looked after **Ara** and later her daughter, **Kaylifa,** to grow the **Aramis Family** which included the exciting **Kaylif,** who sadly met his death in a training yard accident before he could reach his full potential; **Kaylina,** the last and the sweetest of the family, not forgetting the brilliant **Zayfire Aramis** who proved himself to be a winning horse, worthy of the name of his sire, **Zafeen,** and the connection with **Kayf Tara.**

Barbara Coltman

<u>KAYF ARAMIS</u>
There is indeed magic in a name

Kayf *Tara*

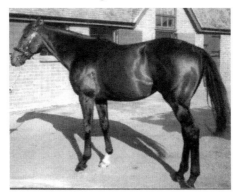

Ara

Mis*ty*

For the life and adventures of Misty go to Part 3

Bertie, Kaylina and Kayfi at home

Part 1 Reflections on the Malvern Hills

Isobel Coltman

Malvern Hills Ride

The Malvern Hills rise peacefully ahead, like a sleeping dragon in the early misty morning. The air is crisp, fresh tasting; the ground still frosty. Golden sunlight highlights the top of the ridge and wispy clouds beckon. Kayfi and I set off on our magical ride.

Our shadow, a length in front, dances on the grass verge, leading the way up the hill towards the common. As the shadow moves up the hedge, Kayfi raises his head and snorts, shying at the shadow; he's ready to race.

"Steady, Kayfi."

One, two, three four. At the sound of Kayfi's steady hoofbeats on the road, three horses lift their heads from grazing. Kayfi jogs, keen to run. The horses come to the hedge to see who is walking past their field, but they don't want to race. Sheep scatter ahead of us. No one wants to race. "*Beautiful morning.*" A lady with two large black dogs stops to let us past, the dogs restrained by their leashes. "*Is he a youngster?*" she asks as Kayfi dances away from the dogs.

Turning onto the common, we catch up with the shadow. Kayfi's hoofbeats are now muffled on the grass.

"*Come on,*" says the shadow "*let's race!*"

Kayfi pricks his ears. Shortening the reins, I lean forwards slightly and Kayfi springs into a canter. We're off and racing! Kayfi swings easily along in a good rhythm, moving upsides the shadow. The wind in our face, we race the shadow up the hill.

In my mind's eye, we are at Cheltenham racecourse, racing up the hill towards the winning post. We've taken the lead and, with the roar of the crowd cheering us on, we power on up the hill.

"*Come on, Kayfi!*" I call to my willing mount. Kayfi's ears flick out to the side, listening to me, and I feel his power as his stride lengthens and he stretches out his neck, his hooves thundering on the grass. We are out in front by a length and a half to the shadow...

Isobel on Kayf Aramis

Cheltenham Festival 10 Years Ago

"Out in front Kayf Aramis and Aidan Coleman, they go for home by just over a length to Buena Vista in second... Kayf Aramis is over the final flight with a lead of a length and a half over Buena Vista in second... They've got 150 yards to go. Kayf Aramis is looking for the line, still out in front by a length and a half to Buena Vista, who is trying to edge back..."

(Racecourse commentary Cheltenham 12th March 2009)

Aidan Coleman on Kayf Aramis at Cheltenham 2009
Photo courtesy Grossick Photography

It's day three of the Cheltenham Festival, the most important race meeting in the calendar, the Olympics of jump racing. Top horses from UK and Ireland are competing in 28 races this week for Festival glory. The dream of every trainer, jockey and owner is to have a winner at Cheltenham.

The second race of the day, the Pertemps Final, is one of the most competitive handicaps of the week. It is run over a gruelling three miles, with qualifiers being held throughout the year. Amongst the 22 runners is Kayf Aramis, entered by his trainer Venetia Williams, as "a social runner," after winning his last two races and getting into the race on bottom weight. He will be ridden by young, talented jockey Aidan Coleman, who is not expecting Kayfi to win this competitive race as it is a huge step up in class.

At Venetia Williams' picturesque training yard in rural Herefordshire, just 30 miles from Cheltenham, Kayf Aramis is getting excited. He's pacing around his box. He can sense that it's race day. Kayfi's lass has been hard at work since dawn. Haggis (when we first met she said: "I'm Elaine, but everyone calls me Haggis") has already mucked out her string, ridden two, then taken Kayfi out to stretch his legs and have a pick of grass. Now, she's grooming him and plaiting his mane and tail, making him look smart for the biggest race of his life.

"I remember Bells coming out to say he got in the Pertemps and said he was the social runner. I said to Bells that he would surprise them all as he was flying." says Haggis.

Haggis has looked after Kayfi since he joined Venetia's yard at the beginning of the season. Haggis is the most important person in Kayfi's life. She's the one that looks after him, rides him every day and knows him so well.

Haggis on Kayfi at Venetia Williams yard

Half an hour from Cheltenham, in the small, peaceful Gloucestershire village of Ashleworth, Gary and I are at the fields where Kayfi's family live out all year round.

Zayfi

Kayfi's sister has a handsome one-week-old chestnut colt foal. Zayfi is Kaylifa's first foal by Royal Ascot winner Zafeen. Born in the middle of the night, I had to pull him out as he was so big and then he took a long time to get up as his legs are so long.

Ross with Zayfi

We let Kaylifa and Zayfi out into the field for a run round where they are greeted by Ara, dam of Kayf, Kaylifa and Kaylif Aramis. I clean out the field shelter while Gary gets fresh straw and changes the water, and 6-year-old Ross, (luckily a day off school) gets the hay, more over himself than in the shelter.

As we work, we're already starting to feel pre-race nerves.

This is Kayfi's 46th race, and we've been to all of them, but this is not like any race we have been to before. This is the Cheltenham Festival.

"The best we can hope for is top six in this field" says Gary.

"I'll be happy with top six." I say.

"Kayfi doesn't know who he's running against. If you put him up against better horses, he always runs better," says Gary.

"Come on Kaylifa, time to come back in for your feed. We have to get to Cheltenham to watch Kayfi race,"

Kaylifa leads her foal safely back into the field shelter and tucks into her feed.

"See you later. Good luck to Kayfi" his family appear to say as we leave them in peace and quiet and head for the noisy crowds of the Cheltenham Festival.

My Mum and Dad are already at Cheltenham, having left London early to avoid traffic.

My Mum, recovering from a recent triple heart bypass, and going to the Cheltenham Festival would not be considered the best rehab, takes up the commentary:

Mum:

"Even I, with so little exposure to racing, feel the air heavy with excitement and expectation with the roar of the crowd signalling the end of the first race. Next one up, The Pertemps Final, Kayfi's race. My heart beat is up. Look at the line up! There are 22 horses, mostly from UK and Ireland. Real bruisers with matching names. How will our Kayfi fare amongst this lot? There is no expectation of a win, I know, because we have just spoken to Venetia, as always, impeccably and elegantly dressed, and she says that this is a social run, so, "Be still" my heart!

In the parade ring now. Here comes Kayfi, looking calm and composed and beautifully groomed and led proudly by Haggis.

"Nobody has told him this is just a 'social run'." Isobel whispers *"He doesn't know he is racing horses higher rated than him. To him they are all, well, just horses to run against."*

The jockeys are now weaving their way through the crowd. The sharp green and white silks find our little crowd of Venetia, Isobel, Gary, Derek, her father, and me holding on to Ross's hand. He looks like a miniature of Aidan Coleman.

Last minute instructions.

"Good luck! Good Luck! Come back safe!"

The jockeys mount and off they go in a line, we follow as well as we can and see Kayfi taking off at a canter towards the starting line.

Here we are in the stands crushed among the crowds.

They're off!

The noise doesn't abate...We strain to catch sight of the green and white colours.

There he is! Jumping well all in a cacophony of colours and sound rising to a pitch as they come for the home run. Unbelievable! Kayfi has beaten off the opposition and here he is powering up that hill with Buena Vista in his wake.

"...the Pertemps Final goes to Kayf Aramis!"

I hear the commentator say and "*Venetia Williams has got her Festival winner,*"

HE'S WON!

IT'S KAYF ARAMIS

My legs have turned to jelly.

Isobel runs off with Ross to walk her winner back into the Winning Paddock together with Haggis and Gary. She babbles excitedly to the cameras.

Derek proudly makes a comment.

Tears well up in my eyes and I see and hear everything through a blur. I know what a big deal this is for my little family, especially Isobel. How improbable that here we are at the pinnacle of the Horse Racing Jumps calendar. I reflect on the journey that started with a pony in my back garden in North London to Kayfi born in a cow shed, now A CHAMPION.

I fight hard to hold back the tears.

Isobel Gary and Ross are now presented with a beautiful trophy.

Can it get any better?"

Aidan Coleman and Kayf Aramis in the Winners Enclosure at Cheltenham
Photo courtesy Grossick Photography

As I fight my way through the crowd into the parade ring looking for Kayfi to come in, clutching tightly onto Ross who is proudly wearing Kayfi's colours, a presenter from Racing UK thrusts a microphone towards me.

"What's it like to have a Festival winner?" he asks.

"He's amazing. He's amazing." I say.
"Winner at Cheltenham is just... I can't believe it. I honestly can't believe it."
"Really, really pleased and it's all thanks to the team, all thanks to Venetia and all the hard work with Haggis."

The crowds are clapping and cheering. Jockey, Aidan Coleman, is saluting the crowd.

"Well done, Kayfi! Best day of my life. Thank you!" I call to Aidan, then looking down at Ross's little face, I feel immediately guilty.

37

Haggis offers me the reins. *"No, let's both lead him in"* I say. Haggis is on the right, I take the left rein, still holding tightly to Ross. Gary is at the rear with Venetia and my parents. We lead Kayfi into the winner's enclosure with Haggis gesturing for the crowd to cheer louder.

Haggis: *"I knew he'd run a good race."*
"I said to Aidan that he would run a big race walking round the paddock and Aidan said if he's in the first 10 he's run a big race. Well, as you know he won and Aidan could hardly speak. He gave Aidan his first Cheltenham festival winner"
"He was a special boy to me and will keep the memories forever"

Aidan: *"I couldn't believe how well that went, you know. He's had a brilliant run through the whole way. Now that he's got his head in front, it seems to have done him the world of good*
Awesome, brilliant, couldn't describe it"

Commentator: *"This will be a day this young man will remember all of his life."*

Commentator:
"What a grand horse Kayf Aramis has been over the years. I remember him winning on desperate ground on the flat at York. He handles all sorts of ground. He's a thorough stayer... He's battled on bravely."

Trainer Venetia Williams:
"He's amazing.
He jumped really well. I think he even showed a change of gear. I just can't believe it! Two runs ago I couldn't even win a maiden hurdle with him! I am so thrilled for Isobel. I think she was totally shocked when I said we might enter him for Cheltenham and even more shocked to discover that we actually got into the race. I should think that she's probably on a stretcher now!"

We are interviewed by Channel 4 Racing.
Interviewer to Ross *"Will you be getting more pocket money now?"*
Later that day, Ross will ask *"What's pocket money?"* Now we're in trouble!

Luckily Ross doesn't remember my Mum promised him the Morgan Aero 8 on display at Cheltenham, that he had sat in earlier in the afternoon, if Kayfi won!

Well the best we thought he'd come was 6th.

After all the excitement of receiving the trophy, I suddenly remember the little foal back home.

"We'd better get back to check on Kaylifa and Zayfi"

Racing is still going on, the muffled sounds of the commentary in the background, but we are in a dream. Proudly carrying the trophy, we make our way through the crowds. On reaching Ashleworth, people wave us down and excitedly congratulate us on our win. Kaylifa neighs as she hears our car pull up at the field. It's so peaceful here, far removed from the events earlier in the day. It almost seems unreal.

Little Zayfi wakes up from a nap in the straw, oblivious to the fact that Uncle Kayfi has just won at the Cheltenham Festival.

"You're going to be a racehorse one day, just like Uncle Kayfi" I tell him.

Nine years later...

Zayfire Aramis wins at Leicester 11th January 2018 for trainer Michael Scudamore with his lass Bella and jockey Tom Scudamore, who was runner-up behind Kayf Aramis at the Cheltenham Festival. Photo courtesy Tony Knapton

Malvern Hills At the Top

After the excitement of racing our shadow, our thoughts turn from Cheltenham back to Elgar's land of hope and glory and the steep climb up to the top of the Malvern Hills. Kayfi trots up the track towards British Camp, the Iron Age hill fort with its extensive earthworks. At the top, Kayfi pricks his ears and takes a breather.

We are greeted by the amazing view of the Severn Valley across to Bredon Hill rising from the mist. Behind stand the Cotswolds, with the highest point Cleeve Hill which forms the spectacular backdrop to Cheltenham racecourse, the scene of Kayfi's greatest success and where he raced a total of 17 times.

From Cheltenham, it's easy to follow the line of the road to Gloucester and then to the small Gloucestershire village of Ashleworth, on the banks of the River Severn. I picture the lovely church of St Andrew and St Bartholomew where Gary and I were married. Ara and Misty were guests of honour at our wedding, looking very smart dressed up in shiny horse brasses and taking a keen interest in my bouquet.

Isobel & Gary on their wedding day with Ara and Misty

Not far from the church is the cowshed where Kayfi was born.

The Cowshed 17 Years Ago

Ara lives at Paul and Mandy's farm in Ashleworth, just down the road from our house. When my beloved pony Misty, died on Midsummer's Day in 2000, Ara was so distraught to lose her long-time companion, that I decided to put her in foal.

Ara is in foal to Kayf Tara, who twice was victorious in the Ascot Gold Cup, owned by Godolphin, and stands at Simon Sweeting's stud farm in Overbury. It is Kayf Tara's first season at stud. This will be Ara's first foal.

Despite being four months pregnant, I have spent the last month watching Ara on night vision camera from a caravan, having read all the books that say horses normally foal at night and at 11 months, not in the morning at 12 months!

Ara's foaling stable is and old disused cowshed on the farm. Gary and I spent time painting the beams black and laying down rubber matting and copious amounts of straw to make it into a super luxury cowshed.

This morning things are different. Ara is looking very uneasy. It must be time. I rush home to fetch Gary, who luckily has a Saturday off work.

"Looks like Ara is almost ready to foal! She just tried to roll," I tell him.

"It's about time!" says Gary.

On our way back to the farm, I call in for Paul, the farmer. *"I'll be right there."*

By the time we get back to Ara, she is looking very restless. She's pacing up and down, pawing at the banks of freshly laid straw. I'm pacing up and down outside, more nervous than Ara.

Paul arrives at the door, then his children peek over the top, then their pony Bracken comes to see what's going on.

Ara is very agitated now, kicking at her belly, then she lies down in the straw and it's time.

"I can see one hoof, but the other one is bent back," I say nervously.

Paul, experienced with sheep and cows, gently straightens the leg. Then, in a whoosh, as if suddenly impatient to come into the world, the long-awaited foal is here. Ara quickly gets to her feet, turning towards the small dark brown figure in the straw, who has one ear bent back, his crumpled body appears too small for his legs. Ara whinnies to her foal, instinctively licking him all over to clean and warm him up.

Ara and new-born Kayfi

Isobel with Ara and Kayfi at four weeks old

Ara and Kayfi at home after retiring from racing

Full Brothers Kaylif and Kayfi at home

Kaylif and Kayfi in training at Nigel Twiston-Davies
with Craig and Becky

Malvern Hills The Ride Home

After reflecting on Kayfi's very modest beginnings in a cowshed in Ashleworth, it's time to head back home.

I give Kayfi an affectionate pat on the neck.

"Good boy, Kayfi."

We set off down the steep path, walking now, enjoying the views. We reach Gullet Quarry and Kayfi stops to look at the reflection of the quarry-face dancing on the water and jackdaws flying overhead.

Turning away from Gullet Quarry, we reach Hollybush common and Mill Pond, where Gary liked to come with friends when he was younger to chill out and talk through the night. We walked here many times together and enjoyed a wonderful picnic here with my Mum and Dad, besides a stream, when Ross was small. I longed, then, to be able to ride a horse here.

Kayfi is now keen to get home. We get back on the road. Our shadow is behind us now and we're on our own again.

"*Neigh!*" I'm on my way, calls out Kayfi to his family waiting down below. "*Neigh!*" We hear the reply across the fields.

Kayfi's hoofbeats quicken now. He's eager to get back to his family
A chorus of neighs greets us as we get back to the field.

"*Neigh!*" We're home, neighs Kayfi.

Kayfi's dam, Ara, his sisters Kaylifa and Kaylina and nephew Bertie crowd around the gate to welcome Kayfi back home.

Kayf Aramis can enjoy a well earned rest and dream about his racing days.

Kayfi at home

Part 2 At the Races

Derek Coltman

On the Level

When Kayf Aramis (Kayfi) reached his second birthday, Isobel had to turn her thoughts to the future and what she planned to do with her elegant animal. Clearly he was going to race but what kind of a race horse would he become. His Sire, Kayf Tara, was a two-mile-plus stayer. Would that be Kayfi's fate? It does seem that horses' genes are much stronger and more influential than the human variety. For if a marathon runner has a son it does not seem to stop the latter from running a 4-minute mile. But with horses it does seem to be the case that the offspring takes on more directly the characteristics of the parents but which one is often a big question. It was presumed, therefore, that Kayfi would be suited to races of distances of more than two miles. That was why it was slightly surprising, I must say with hindsight, that it was decided to place him with a trainer as a 2-year-old. Clearly money played a big part in the decision. It is not cheap to train a race horse, so when Isobel noticed a trainer offering the first three months' training for free, she was tempted and eventually gave in to the temptation.

Kayfi was duly despatched to Ian Wood's yard. His first experience of going into the horse box almost proved to be his last. Whilst being coaxed up the ramp, he pulled back and slipped and fell on his back. Gasps of alarm all round but soon to be followed by sighs of relief as he quickly got to his feet and seemed none the worse for wear. He then proceeded to go quite calmly into the box. So he went off to his new home, visited regularly by devoted family and friends. He seemed to take well to the training and performed well on the twice-weekly gallops. The trainer, therefore, picked out a race for him which took place at Sandown Park on 24th June 2004, when Kayfi was two years and two months old. Technically, of course, he was four months older than reality because race horses have their 'official' birthday on January 1st.

First Race - Sandown

It was an anxious day for the Phipps/ Coltman family, Isobel, Gary and Ross. It would be their first day at the races with their own race horse. The race was a Maiden Stakes for 2-year-olds to be run over seven furlongs. There were twelve runners and Kayfi was allocated stall 6. It was 'fingers crossed' and hope that Kayfi had been well trained on how to emerge from the stalls. The race time came and they were off. Well eleven of them were! A few split seconds ticked by before Kayfi eventually emerged from the stalls, running about sixteen lengths behind all the others. One thing can be said for him, though, he didn't fall any further behind his rivals. He finished 12th or last, officially sixteen lengths behind the winner. His odds for his first race were 50/1 but he was beaten into last place by a 66/1 shot!

Racing Post Comments in Running summed it up thus: **Very slowly away, behind, no chance when veered badly right inside final 3f**
Quite! Ah well. Not a very encouraging debut.

The 'post mortem', however, revealed some interesting, mitigating circumstances. It turned out that 'behind' had a lot to do with it! Kayfi had been frightened by the sudden opening of the stalls (lack of training?), reared up, did a number two and then charged out of the stalls. No wonder he was so far behind! This sounds like excuses. But there are always excuses in racing. The jockey? The ground? The distance? True. But here the distance was a question. His sire was a two-miler-plus stayer and this was seven furlongs. This was a sprint. And as history will reveal, Kayfi doesn't sprint. The jockey? Well. He did whip him a few times which Kayfi was not used to and probably reacted by 'veering badly to the right inside the final three furlongs', as reported. Another interesting outcome is that another trainer, John Spearing, had watched the race and decided that something was wrong with Kayfi. He conveyed his views to Isobel and said that he would take Kayfi into training after the vet had inspected him. This happened almost immediately. Kayfi was fetched and taken to his new home. It turned out later, according to the vet, that Kayfi had been ill with some virus on the day of the race and probably should not have competed. The vet stated also that he would not repeat these opinions publicly because 'you know the racing community'! He also recommended that Kayfi be gelded. This operation seems to be quite common among young stallions whose health is not 100%. Most of them go on to be fully revitalised and have a successful racing career. This was quite a blow for Isobel because she had dreams of Kayfi becoming a Sire of note in the future. But that was not to be. So the upshot is that Kayfi had 'the operation' in the new trainer's yard and he immediately advised that Kayfi should 'go home' and recuperate in the fields for three months. This happened and Kayfi recovered in natural surroundings in a field by Isobel's home in 'mum's' company and became fit enough to return to training in January 2005, officially as a three-year-old.

Four months later he was considered ready to have another go at the racing game. An evening race at Windsor on 9th May was selected. It was again a Class 5 Maiden Stakes event but this time over 10 furlongs (1 mile 2 furlongs). With hindsight, of course, this was also too short a distance for him but Isobel had to trust that the new trainer knew his 'onions', so to speak. Isobel and her family duly gathered at the racecourse and nervously awaited the 8.20. All that can be said about this race is that Kayfi maintained his record and came last. This time his odds were 100/1!

Racing Post had just two words to say: **'Always behind'**
Can't argue with that!! No Number Two this time, though!

Warwick
A month later on 13 June there was yet another Maiden Stakes at Warwick over 13 furlongs. The distance was extending and getting gradually closer to the optimum. It was quite a small race with only 5 runners so there was hope, or so we thought. But he was rated 100/1. Well, it seemed that some kind of pattern was emerging. It reminds me of the old joke about the guy who dreamt he should back horse number 5 in the 5th race and, you guessed it, Kayfi came 5th!! Odds 66/1 in a five-horse race!

Racing Post's comment in running was a master stroke of brevity:
Held up, weakened 5f out

Beverley

The turning point came on 18th July way up in the North of England, in Beverley. This time it was a Maiden Handicap Stakes because Kayfi had completed his mandatory three races and was now officially rated at 45. The distance was two miles (now we're getting to it!) and the going was officially 'Good'. His odds were 25/1 jointly with two others and, what is more, there were at least three horses at higher odds. Were the bookies starting to detect something? The race went very well for Kayfi. He was always in a good position under the control of an excellent jockey, Sam Hitchcott. I'll spare you any further suspense – Kayfi came Third!! Yes he came **THIRD**! What rejoicing and excitement there was among the Coltman family! Third and with prize money to boot, or 'to shoe'!!.

Kayfi 3rd at Beverley with Isobel, Ross and Becky

And what did our dear old **Racing Post** have to say about this fantastic event in Coltman family history?: **Held up towards rear, headway over 6f out, ridden to chase leaders 3f out, driven and kept on same pace approaching final furlong.**

Some people can just not recognise sheer genius when it stares them in the face!

53

Nottingham

Now it seemed time to examine what was happening. What was different? Well, the distance was nearer to his Sire's successful runs. The ground was Good. Previous runs had been Good to Firm. Kayfi was clearly not cut out to be a runner on Good to Firm at this stage of his career, but horses do adapt and change as they get older. It would seem that anything from Good to Softer was going to suit him. This was undoubtedly a milestone for Kayfi on the way to the 'Dream'. Only eleven days later it was decided to run Kayfi again. This time at Nottingham. The distance was two miles and the going was 'Soft'. It was generally thought that he ran a creditable race and came 4th, unfortunately just outside the frame for prize money. But 4th!! We had become used to his finishing in the high numbers but now he was getting 3rds and 4ths. And his odds were in single figures, too – 8/1. He was starting to make his mark. Also of interest are the three horses that beat him: Whoopsie, Pee Jay's Dream and Figaro's Quest. These were to become some of Kayfi's rivals and he would eventually beat them all.

Kayfi 4th at Nottingham with Isobel, Ross and Becky

But we mustn't get too carried away. We have **Racing Post** to consider:

Chased leaders, driven along over 5f, hung left and stayed on one pace final 2f (op 8-1)

Oh well. You can't win 'em all!

REFLECTIONS ON NOTTINGHAM
(Barbara Coltman)

I'm standing in the queue for chocolate covered strawberries for Ross. The lasses are made of sterner stuff - no matter what the weather they turn out in their flimsiest of fineries only goosebumps on their arms

Ross celebrating Kayfi's 4th place

betraying the bitter cold of the day. Nothing can deter them from having FUN! What is more they had chosen Kayf Aramis as the one they were going to put their money on!

It is at Nottingham when something of the beauty of racing clicked in my head. As the horses surged slightly uphill towards the start of the race, the shape of the horses, their manes blowing in the wind, their jockeys perched on top in their colourful silks reminded me of an impressionist painting, by Degas, was it, or a Manet. Just a fleeting glance of perfection!

Chepstow

Chepstow was the next target on the 29th August. Two miles again and the going 'Good'. This seemed to be going against the statistics. On record it was beginning to look as though Kayfi was not cut out for running on 'Good'. We were not too optimistic. But there were thirteen runners and the bookies rated him again an 8/1 chance. Well, Kayfi produced another 4th! Quite a satisfactory performance, considering the ground. What is more, he beat one of the trio of horses mentioned earlier – Figaro's Quest. One down and two to go! That was pleasing.

What's that you say? Oh. What did **Racing Post** comment?:
Chased leaders, hard driven over 3f out, soon outpaced
What did you expect? It took a long time for **Racing Post** to even really notice Kayfi, let alone say anything favourable.

Becky with Kayfi at Chepstow

Gary and Ross

Pontefract

3rd October 2005 proved the start of a long 'love-hate' relationship with Pontefract or 'Bloody Pontefract', as certain members of the Coltman family began to call it. This had nothing to do with that lovely medieval town in West Yorkshire, before its inhabitants rise up and march on London! It was because we were to have so many frustrating experiences there. Seconds and Thirds but never Firsts! "Always the bridesmaid, never the bride" as the saying goes. It's 170 miles from London and that's a long way home when Kayfi hasn't done what was expected, i.e. won. No-one speaks. No stops are made. Just get home three hours later. And a large whisky or two to drown the frustration! This time the distance was two miles one furlong – slowly getting there! The ground was 'Soft'. Kayfi had acquired extra weight, courtesy the handicapper, for his couple of 3rds and 4ths and was now on 53. He also had another jockey, Frankie McDonald, to get used to. There were fourteen runners. The less said the better really. He came 8th and was rated a 25/1 shot. I should gloss over what our favourite racing paper wrote but we might as well hear the worst because things can get better -and they do!

Chased leaders, hung left and lost place 2f out

'Lost place' – crowded out by the other more experienced jockeys more like it!

Kayfi at Pontefract
with Frankie McDonald

Pontefract

And two weeks later on 17th October we did it all over again. Kayfi was entered in a 2-mile, 2-furlong contest, the toteexacta Bluff Cove Handicap. The handicapper had been really generous in the light of his previous run and lightened the load by three pounds to 50. There was also another change of jockey. This time it was Paul Quinn. This was the start of a year's consistent relationship with Kayfi and the beginning of the turning of the tide. Or perhaps, as Churchill might have said – "the beginning of the beginning". For Kayfi came 6th out of 11 runners. Not exactly disgraced even at 40/1 but not entirely bathed in any, even reflected, glory, either.

RP is starting to sound like an abbreviation for **'Rest (in) Peace'!:**
In touch, ridden along over 4f out, plugged on same pace
This 'same' or 'one pace' was becoming to be a bit of an **RP** trade mark for Kayfi. They didn't realise yet that he doesn't have a sprint but keeps on running determinedly.

Bath

Bath race course is the highest track in the UK. We had no idea what significance this had until it was decided as Kayfi's next challenge. That was to be on 11th April 2006 when he was officially a Four-year-old. Before that, however, Kayfi was given a well-earned rest back home in the muddy field for a couple of months. Then it was back to work. Race Day duly arrived. – the ninth race in Kayfi's short life. The ground was 'Soft', the distance 2 miles, 1 furlong, fourteen runners and Paul Quinn in the saddle. Kayfi's odds were 28/1, so not much has changed there. The weather was abysmal. Heavy clouds and continuous rain. Now the consequences of being the 'highest race course in the UK' were revealed. Clouds and mist had descended over the course and the track was barely visible. We saw the start of the race with Kayfi going off in the lead, which he had never really done before. Then all the horses disappeared into the murky haze. The large viewing screen just looked grey. The commentator continued valiantly even though he hadn't a clue what was happening. At one point he said; "By my watch they should be half-way but, if anyone spots them before me, let me know!' We did glimpse murky figures from time to time but could not make out who was who. We stood in the grandstand overlooking the winning post. The rain was still bucketing down. We had seen Kayfi so often and been disappointed when he started out well and then was overtaken towards the end of the race by the 'sprinters'. We just expected the usual and the worst. We looked into the swirling mist in anticipation. I felt like Bobbie (played by Jenny Agutter) in the film, 'The Railway Children', whose father has been wrongly imprisoned for a number of years for spying. At the close of the story Bobbie has an uncanny feeling that something unexpected is going to happen. She hurries down to the station. She doesn't know why. Bernard Cribbins, the friendly stationmaster, yells something, pointing to a newspaper headline as he rushes to deal with the incoming train. Bobbie doesn't understand. She looks at the train that has just arrived. She is standing on the platform with everyone and everything hidden by swirling steam. She stares into the mist and cannot make out anything. Time seems to stand still. It is silent. Then suddenly the steam clears away and there stands a man. 'Daddy, my Daddy!' Bobbie cries as she runs to embrace her returning father.

I, too, stared into the mist. I hardly dared to hope. There was an eerie silence as if something was about to happen. But what? The mist stopped roughly a hundred yards from the winning post. The commentator had almost given up but said he thought he saw something! And they should be coming into sight soon!! Then silence. The suspense was tortuous. All the Coltman family were, if they were honest, not expecting great things. Except perhaps Isobel. She was always optimistic and thought the best of everyone and everything. The song 'The impossible dream' could have been written for her. Particularly the line 'To reach the unreachable star'. It seemed like an age went by. I descended the steps to get closer to the track. The silence was almost deafening. It was still raining. It was eerily quiet. I stared into the mist. I didn't know what to expect. Then: 'Kayfi, my Kayfi!' I knew how Bobbie felt on seeing what emerged from the gloom! Kayfi came galloping out of the mist, in the lead, just as he was at the start.
I heard the commentator say: "And Kayf Aramis is the winner. Lord knows how!"

What had happened in between is anyone's guess. He had won his first race and we only saw the last hundred yards of his triumph. That didn't seem fair but he had won. Everyone in the family was ecstatic, particularly Isobel and Gary, who stood in the winner's enclosure, rain streaming down their faces but with beaming smiles that would have melted icebergs. He opened at 33/1 and closed at 28/1. The bookies were adamant to the end. Out of family loyalty, crazily, I had placed a bet of £60 at 30/1 – and won

£1800! The biggest win of my life. It certainly compensated me for all the previous occasions when I had carried out similar acts of loyalty with no such profitable outcome. Kayfi made his owner some good money at last but it was the win that counted above all rewards

Kayfi Winner at Bath with Paul Quinn, Isobel, Derek, Becky and Gary

Oh - and the racing rag commented:

Made virtually all, ridden over 4f out, held on well

A slight change of tune, though short of full praise for a job well done. 'Held on well' they begrudgingly commented. Still couldn't bring themselves to utter the word **'WON'**! Kayfi's first triumph on his ninth career outing with already one Third and two Fourths to his credit.

Gary, Isobel and Ross with Kayfi at Bath

Pontefract

Just under two weeks later, on 24th April, Kayfi was running in the Pontefract Marathon Handicap. Now you are talking! Two miles and five furlongs. This is getting to be a distance where Kayfi can demonstrate his staying powers. Twelve runners but ground Good. Not the best of omens. Paul Quinn on board. Kayfi ran very well in this race. He was leading three furlongs to go and was pipped to the post at the end by one-and-three-quarter lengths. But a very creditable result. Our journey back to London was not so taciturn or sad. There was conversation that was full of 'what ifs'. 'What if Kayfi had lengthened his stride and headed for home four furlongs out. What if ....what if....' But he came 2nd and we were grateful for that.

Racing Post:

Fly-jumped start, held up in rear, pushed along and headway 6f out, led 3f out until just inside final furlong, kept on same pace

' ... kept on same pace' – haven't we heard that somewhere before?

Kayfi 2nd at Pontefract
with Paul Quinn

Kayfi at Pontefract with Isobel,
Ross and Becky

60

York – Winner!

On 18th May 2006 a decision was made to run Kayfi at York – another track miles away in the North of England. Omens looked good. The Sportsman Racing Stakes. Distance 2 miles 4 furlongs. He had just acquitted himself with a good run at Pontefract over 2 miles 5 furlongs so this was in his favour. The ground was officially soft – another plus. Quinn riding again so everything familiar. It was an exciting day for the whole family. It was a chilly sort of day with weak sunshine. I cannot recall whether it was Ladies' Day but certainly all the fairer sex were 'dressed to the nines', defying the chill in strapless, low-cut dresses. Kayfi was 9/1 this time. Not such an outsider. He was to meet up with three horses who would on other occasions see his heels disappearing into the distance: Overstrand, Monolith and Great As Gold.

The race started and he ... how did **RP** put it?:
'Held up towards rear, headway halfway, effort on wide outside 3f out, ridden to lead 1f out, stayed on'
Not exactly gushing with praise but it is **Racing Post!**

What the reporter is really trying to say but the words won't come out, is that Kayfi **WON**! By one-and-a-half lengths! He **WON** a two-and-a-half mile race on **Soft ground**. He **WON** and started what became a short-lived trend of coming from the back of the field to make his strike. Paul Quinn was the jockey at the time. And Overstrand, Monolith and Great As Gold finished Second, Third and Fourth, respectively!

But the trainer, John Spearing, well known for not wasting his words, responded to Isobel's congratulatory telephone call with "There you are then!"

Kayfi winner at York with Paul Quinn
Isobel and Ross

York (Barbara Coltman)

I was left looking after little Ross, resplendent in his green/white silks, chasing him around a tree when a young man studying the race programme, a Nigel Havers look-alike, approached and seeing Ross asked if Kayf Aramis was his horse. "Yes, " replied Ross. "Do you think he'll win" "Indeed" said I confidently, "That's why we're here" Off went the young man to put money on Kayf Aramis on our say-so. Ross and I didn't even get to see the race but could hear the roar of the crowd and soon everyone was coming back in a great wave back to the bookies to claim their money or to the paddocks to take a look at the next contestants. In the crowd I saw the young man fighting his way through towards us, waving his programme excitedly. He came to thank us! He has no idea how much we appreciated that gesture, so, if you, Mr Nigel Havers look-alike, are reading this, do get in touch!

Pontefract

25th June saw us once again driving North to Pontefract! The only slightly worrying aspect of the race was that the ground was Good to Firm – not Kayfi's favourite condition, although he did later seem to change his reaction and perform quite well. The usual suspects were there – Overstrand and Monolith. We were reasonably confident. His odds were about 4/1. As the race progressed I got nervous and the old visions of failure flashed before my eyes. Kayfi seemed to be holding back unduly in the rear. It made me wonder whether Quinn was trying to reproduce the York success of coming from the back of the field. This was not normally Kayfi's way as he does not have a real sprint. He's a stayer and can outrun any rival, given the right conditions of ground and distance. Unfortunately these two requisites were not present in equal values and, in my opinion, Quinn got it wrong. Kayfi finished 5th out of a seven-horse field!

This time **Racing Post** was not so far wrong:
Held up in rear, effort and some headway 3f out, soon ridden along and never a factor.
Held up in the rear. Exactly!

Kempton

The next race was a strange one. The trainer, John Spearing, decided to run Kayfi on the all-weather track at Kempton on 2nd August. Strange decision not only because of the ground but the distance – just two miles which was a bit short for Kayfi. Anyway, after a slow start, Kayfi did actually manage to get into the lead by the sixth furlong. Then something unusual happened. He lurched to the left on the bend. We were at first not sure what had happened but it eventually became clear. The way back to the stables was just across from the bend. Kayfi probably thought he had done enough by then and he would prefer to go back to the stables. He couldn't make any progress after that upset and finished 7th out of 12. This was to be Kayfi's one-and-only venture into all-weather racing. The result stands out like a sore thumb on his career record.

As our old friend **Racing Post** put it so succinctly:
Slowly away but soon led, faltered on bend after 7f, headed soon after, never on terms but made some late headway

Pontefract
Eighteen days later, on 20th August, saw us all on the way back to Pontefract for a two-miler on Good ground. Old rivals were also there: Mr. Arjay, Rose Bien and Thewhirlingdervish. Paul Quinn was the jockey again and once more we saw Kayfi held up at the back. We were definitely starting to think that this had become Quinn's strategy – repeating the York success by winning from the rear. Well it didn't work again and Kayfi came 5th in a field of nine. This was beginning to be annoying!!

Ross

Newcastle

On 28th August we, Southerners, made the long trek northwards to Newcastle for a two-mile race on Good to Soft ground. Another future rival appeared in this seven-horse race – Numero Due - who would give Kayfi a run for his money on more than one occasion. This was not to be Kayfi's race again. He came 5th!

And what do you think **RP** had to say?
Took keen hold in rear, reminders 10f out, soon chasing leaders, lost place over 1f out

'Took keen hold in the rear' – eh!! Once more the old 'win-from-the-back' strategy. It was starting to become patently obvious that Paul Quinn was determined to ride this way despite evidence to the contrary that it was really not Kayfi's strength. This was, in fact, Paul Quinn's last ride on Kayfi. This was a pity because he had produced two firsts and a second from eight rides. No mean accomplishment and we were grateful, even though it didn't look like it, as he was dropped as Kayfi's jockey.

Warwick

A new jockey was selected in an effort to change Kayfi's racing strategy. This was Steve Drowne and the track was to be Warwick – and not so far for the Southern clan to travel. The date was 4th September. The ground Good and the distance two miles. I always thought that a bit short for Kayfi but he surprised us. He stayed on valiantly with the leader and even went in front for a while. We got a bit excited and dared to hope. But he was pipped at the post. The official result was a 'short head'. Wow! They don't come much closer than that! Two of his old rivals, Rose Bien and Our Monogram were way back in the field. It looked like Steve Drowne had quickly got the hang of how to ride Kayfi.

Kayfi 2nd at Warwick with Steve Drowne

Racing Post was a bit laconic with its comments in running:
With leader, led 7f out , ridden over 2f out, headed near finish
'Headed near finish' gives an idea of how close it was.

Goodwood

Six days later on 10th September Kayfi made his first appearance at Goodwood in a 2-miler where the ground was officially 'Good to Firm'. This latter fact was a little worrying but Isobel was confident that Kayfi could handle these conditions. She even went on to say that she had the impression that Kayfi was changing and was reacting positively to firmer ground. We were about to find out. The other interesting factor to note about this race is that it was a flat race for National Hunt jockeys. The trainer, John Spearing, commented that he wanted to see "how Kayfi managed with a long-legged jockey, used to riding with longer stirrups." The 'long-legged' jockey in question was Paddy Brennan who rode Kayfi for the first time. The race went very well and Kayfi put on a marvellous display and was the only one chasing Kanpai from about half-way. He kept on valiantly but he was no match for the winner's end sprint and finished 2nd, three-and-a-half lengths down. A good race though. No disgrace whatsoever.

Kayfi 2nd at Goodwood with Paddy Brennan

RP thought so, too, but resisted getting too excited about it!

Chased winner from halfway, hard driven over 2f out, kept on but always held
'Kept on but always held' is praise indeed from this illustrious journal.

Warwick

No peace for the weak head, to coin a phrase! Kayfi is working hard. Six days later on 16th. September he's back at Warwick in another 2-miler with the ground 'Good to Soft'. The ground is certainly more in his favour and I am starting to believe Isobel when she says that she thinks Kayfi is adapting more to a shorter distance. Again a switch of jockey – Marc Halford. John Spearing sounds reasonably confident, though, true to character, he doesn't say much. As usual Kayfi ran quite a good race and stayed 'handy', as they say. He was with the action until halfway and then went into the lead until about one furlong out. Then, of course, the old problem arises. He doesn't have a sprint. His main talent is to outrun and outstay the field. It looked as if he might just be able to pull it off but another regular 'sparring partner', Numero Due, decided not to settle with his registered name and became 'Numero Uno'! Kayfi held on and finished one-and-a-quarter lengths down. Nevertheless an admirable performance with the third horse about two lengths behind.

Our favourite racing paper wasn't so enthusiastic, of course:

With leader until led halfway, ridden and headed over 1f out, every chance inside final furlong, unable to quicken

Unable to quicken'. How many times will these words be written before Kayfi comes to the end of his career?

Kayfi 2nd at Warwick with Marc Halford

66

York

It was then decided that it was time to go back to York to defend his reputation. On 7 October 2006 there was a two-mile-two-furlong race and the ground looked like it would be to Kayfi's liking. Another change of jockey, though, and this time it was Kerrin McEvoy – no mean jockey and in his prime. In the ring we dispensed the usual instructions: 'Keep him handy in the 3-4 slot and just keep him running as he does not have a sprint'. He has to outrun the opposition'. We should have it put on an MP3 or something and played it before every race! Anyway all seemed to be going well. He kept up with the leaders and challenged for leadership three furlongs from the end but then seemed to lose it and four horses passed him, leaving him fifth. The only consolation was that he beat Som Tala, Mceldowney and Dr. Sharp. But we were disappointed, particularly with lack of progress in the final furlong. The jockey seemed to be just perching motionless on Kayfi's back. He certainly wasn't urging him on. We met McEvoy on the way in and what did he say? "The others passed him and he couldn't catch them up!" Then he added something that damned him completely in all our eyes: "Let's face it. He's always going to come up against horses that are better than him! "He's got no class". " Not only had he not followed instructions but demeaned our Kayfi into the bargain! That was one jockey who would never again bestride the Coltman pride and joy.

Our old friend, **Racing Post**, was not as harsh as usual and made the following comment:
Always prominent, smooth headway 4f out, disputed lead 3f out, soon ridden and weakened 2f out

Pontefract

On 16 October 2006 we had another chance to go back to Pontefract. We hadn't been there for nearly two whole months and were starting to have withdrawal symptoms! The ground turned out to be Good to Soft. The jockey was an 'old' friend, Marc Halford, who, at that time, was able to claim three pounds, which was all in Kayfi's favour. The race went very well and, as planned, Marc Halford went for it about a mile out and was in the lead half a mile from the winning post but, at one furlong from home, he was caught and passed by Sir Mark Prescott's bay gelding, Esprit de Corps with Seb Sanders aboard. The winning distance was three-and-a-half lengths but Kayfi was four lengths clear of his old rival, Great as Gold, and well ahead of Mr Arjay and The Whirlingdervish. So on the sixth race at Pontefract the winning slot eluded him yet again. So the score to-date was - 8-6-2-5-5-2. Would he ever get that cherished first place at our favourite place in West Yorkshire? On the way back, it was not much later than 5pm, we decided to drive into Pontefract to buy some of the celebrated Pontefract cakes to cheer ourselves up and support the local economy. Alas, the Market Square was deserted and the shops closed. We asked a young man who was hurrying by in the gusty wind where we could get something to eat. His instructions took us back onto the Motorway!

Racing Post:
Tracked leader, challenged 8f out, led 5f out until over 1f out, kept on same pace
In other words he doesn't have a final sprint! Haven't we heard that somewhere before?

Newmarket
John Spearing decided next to run Kayfi at Newmarket on 27 October 2006. This was a new venue and we were not sure why he was being sent there. But we hoped that the trainer had some master plan. This was an interesting day out as we had not been to this racecourse before. It is the home of racing after all. It was a short trip for those living in London but for Isobel, Gary and Ross it was, of course, much further. My sister, Susan, and my brother-in-law, Bill, keen supporters of Kayfi, bravely decided to make the long trip from Huddersfield. It was a pleasant day and we were looking forward to seeing what Kayfi would be able to do in this two-mile event. The ground was suitable, being good to soft so there was no excuse. There were sixteen runners and the one to beat was Dr Sharp. Kayfi ran very well and was always 'handy' as they say in the trade. Dr Sharp made most of the running but Kayfi chased him bravely and as far as four furlongs out it looked as though he had a good chance. He kept on valiantly and was only beaten into **second place** by one-and-a-quarter lengths. This was a good run.

Kayfi 2nd at Newmarket with Marc Halford, Becky, Isobel and Ross

And what does you-know-who comment?:

Always prominent, chased winner over 4f out, soon ridden, edged right over 1f out, kept on.

Not bad! None of the ' running at one pace' or ' didn't have a sprint'. He actually 'kept on'!

Even **Racing Post** was starting to be nice about Kayfi! Now that's progress!

Bath

There was now a long winter break before his next run. We had time to think about the year past and what the future held in store. For whatever reason, on 11 April 2007 it was decided to return to the scene of Kayfi's first great triumph – Bath. This was a two-mile-one-furlong race but the ground was listed as firm – Not ideal for Kayfi but maybe John Spearing knew something we didn't know. So it was off again to Somerset where the weather was very different from the last time. You will remember that Kayfi won his first race in the pouring rain and mist, which was so thick we didn't actually see the race. We were reasonably confident, however, as Kayfi had won there last time. It was an exciting race and Kayfi lead all the way until about three furlongs out and then it was all over. At about the two furlong mark he was passed by four others. So he came fifth, about eight lengths behind the winner. A disappointing race. A miserable journey home.

Our friend, **RP**, laconic as ever:

Led until 3f out, weakened over 2f out

The Coltman family with Uncle Bill and Auntie Sue watching Kayfi at Bath

Newbury

Ten days later, on 21 April, Kayfi made his first trip to Newbury. A Pertemps Handicap, two miles with a ground good to firm. The Jockey was Steve Drowne who had ridden Kayfi twice before. I was a little worried about the ground but Isobel was of the opinion that Kayfi would be all right. I was also concerned that the distance was too short but once again a positive Isobel thought that Kayfi could handle it. The race went quite well and for a while I began to feel that Isobel was right. About half a mile from the finish he even challenged the leader who was a horse Kayfi would come up against a few times afterwards, Junior. Then he seemed to run out of steam and others passed him in the final furlong and he finished ninth in the end. Whether it was the distance or the ground it was not sure. These are always excuses made after each race.

For once I agreed with the comments in running by the **Racing Post**: **Chased winner, challenged from 4f out until over 2f out, weakened final furlong**

York – Winner!

Next it was decided that a return to York on 17 May 2007, perhaps to lay the ghost of the last ride where Kayfi had only managed to come fifth. This time it was the Robert Pratt Memorial Stakes (Handicap). The distance was 2 miles 2 furlongs (a better distance) and the ground was listed as good to soft. So the prospects looked good. Kayfi seemed to like the track at York. He was also known as a 'regular' and so a bit of a celebrity you might say. And there also were a couple of old rivals in the race, Great as Gold and Rose Bien. It looked like quite a challenging competition and because it was the scene of earlier triumphs for Kayfi, we were really looking forward to going there. It was a pleasant day, a little sun, but not too warm. Kayfi duly appeared in the pre-parade ring, led by his proud groom, Becky. She ate and slept horses and Kayfi was a special favourite. She had told us on previous occasions that she could hardly sleep the night before a race. Often she would go to check on Kayfi in the middle of the night. Anyway, she was leading him around the parade ring, as if he were already the champion. The jockey was once more Marc Halford so we were expecting great things. Events moved on, and we went to the official parade ring. John Spearing's instructions were nothing special. Halford was to keep him 'handy' which is racing jargon for being positioned in the first three. The race went very well, and the jockey, followed his instructions to the letter.

At four furlongs out Marc pushed Kayfi into the lead. We hoped he had not gone too soon. We were not sure that Kayfi liked being on his own and, to be sure, when he was about one furlong from the finish, he veered wildly to the right, as if he wanted the company of the other horses. He kept going, however, and beat his old rival, Great as Gold, by one and a quarter lengths. He had done it! He had won again at York.

Kayf winning at York with Marc Halford

We were all in the winners' enclosure, very excited. Isobel was presented with a wonderful trophy in memory of Robert Pratt. Then we went off to have a glass of champagne and watch a video of the race. The journey home was a pleasure this time. No ifs or buts or what ifs. Just going over and relishing the triumphant moments of the race. Shortly after leaving York one of the party, who shall remain nameless, insisted on stopping for a cup of coffee. The first place we came to was a McDonald's. OK, not the most prestigious location to conclude such an exciting and important day. No matter. We'd get a quick coffee and be back on the road without wasting any more time. Looking out of the window, however, we noticed a horsebox pulling up. Minutes later in comes Kayfi's support team to pick up a takeaway. They looked askance at us for 'celebrating' Kayfi's victory at McDonald's, of all places!

Racing Post summed it up like this:
Chased leaders, led over 4f out, edged right over 1f out, stayed on well
'Stayed on well'. Yes, he bloody well did! **He won!**

Isobel and Ross receiving the trophy at York

Goodwood

Maybe the last triumph went to the trainer's head. Seven days later, Kayfi was entered for a race at Goodwood. As far as I was concerned, two things appeared not to be right: the distance was two miles and the ground was good, which means fast. Of course, Kayfi had run there before, on 6 September 2006 when the ground was good to firm and he had come second. So perhaps my fears were groundless. We stood in the hot sun watching Kayfi walk round the parade ring. Marc Halford was riding again. This was not Kayfi's race, however, so say no more!

I hardly dared check **Racing Post** when I got home:
Chased leaders, every chance and ridden 4f out, weakened 3f out
They were half kind for a change. 'Every chance' they said. I wasn't so sure.

Pontefract

Kayfi was given a month's rest after all his exertions. So he was next entered for a two-mile-two- furlong race on the 24 June - at Pontefract! We hadn't been there since the previous October. This would be our seventh visit. Surely a win was in order. Finally. This race was the Pontefract Cup and Kayfi had got to have a good chance of winning. The ground was officially good to soft. The distance was okay. Marc Halford was once more on board. Good omens all round. Old rivals, Great as Gold, and Monolith and also Thewhirlingdervish. This was an exciting race. Kayfi led all the way until the final four furlongs. He was really doing well and it appeared that he had every chance of winning. This was a different Kayfi. We hadn't really seen him run from the front, since his win at Bath (which

Kayfi 3rd at Pontefract with Marc Halford

we didn't see because of mist!). Then, towards the final two furlongs, he was caught by Thewhirlingdervish and Great as Gold and finished 3rd. It was a little disappointing but it was a great effort, and even coming third in such company, was quite something. But he maintained his record of not winning at Pontefract!

Racing Post was as laconic as ever:
Led until 4f out, kept on same pace final 2f

Warwick

Trainer, John Spearing, seemed to like Warwick for some reason or he was determined that Kayfi should at last notch up a win at the West Midlands track as his last two appearances there produced Seconds. So on 6th July we all assembled to watch our hero line up in the Sponsor At Warwick Racecourse Handicap with only six runners. The trip was two miles and the ground was heavy. Marc Halford was back in the saddle for the seventh time looking for a third winner. Despite the shorter distance and heavy conditions, Kayfi really did well and looked as though he could make it. In the end he was only one-and-and-three-quarter lengths behind the winner, Last Flight, ridden by Kerrin McEvoy. You know, the jockey who had the cheek to pronounce: "Let's face it. He's always going to come up against horses that are better than him!" Grrrr!

We had an amusing experience as we left the racetrack. We usually only watched Kayfi run and then would go home. There was a race in progress as we made our way to the car park, quite close to the track. We could hear the cheering crowds a couple of hundred yards away but where we were was relatively quiet. Then suddenly we were bombarded by the sudden noise of a dozen horses or so coming round the last bend before the straight. Then we heard what a racegoer would normally not hear amidst the yells of the crowds cheering on their favourite to win: the jockeys were cursing and swearing loudly –" Sh*t – come on you bugger! Fu**! Bloody hell"! as they urged their mounts to make a last effort.

And **Racing Post**:
Held up, headway halfway, ridden and every chance 1f out, stayed on same pace
'Stayed on same pace'! You don't say!

Beverley

Trainer, John Spearing, had obviously been doing his homework, trying to find a suitable race. So for the next outing on 17 July he opted for the Class 4 122nd Year of The Watt Memorial Handicap at Beverley. Marc Halford was once more chosen to be in the saddle. Yet again Kayfi was up against his old rivals, Thewhirlingdervish and Great as Gold. Kayfi was at the rear of the field for the first three furlongs but then started to show some spirit when making attempts to catch the leaders, Serpentaria, trained by Sir Mark Prescott, and Tim Easterby's Thewhirlingdervish, the eventual winner. Kayfi moved into third position about one furlong from home but couldn't hold it and ended up fourth behind Great As Gold. So beaten once more by his old rivals!

Racing Post was unusually neutral with its comments

Held up, headway to chase leaders over 4f out, went 3rd over 1f out, one pace

Can't disagree with that!

York

There's one thing for sure. John Spearing doesn't believe in allowing his horses to stand idle in field or stable. He decided just eleven days later that another trip to York was called for and entered Kayfi in the Skybet.com Stakes on 28 July. Marc Halford's services were once more in demand. The Coltman family duly congregated at one of their favourite tracks in the North. The distance was two miles two furlongs but the going was heavy. Kayfi was also heavy (9-5), one of three heaviest in the nine-runner field. Interestingly the first three places went to the lighter horses: 1st - Galileo Figaro (9.1), 2nd Last Flight (8.00) 3rd Establishment (8.10). Kayfi came Fifth.

Racing Post gave a fair version:
Soon tracking leaders, joined leader over 7f out, not much room over 2f out, weakened final furlong

Goodwood

Three days later it was back to Goodwood for the third time of asking. Last time, you may recall, Kayfi didn't exactly cover himself with glory, coming thirteenth out of fifteen runners. On the previous occasion, though, he ran a good race and was runner-up. This time it was the Invesco Perpetual Goodwood Stakes over two-and-a-half-miles. The going was listed as 'Good'. An old 'friend', Great As Gold, was one of the runners. Another Quinn – Jimmy - was booked. This jockey didn't keep him at the back of the field but rode our Kayf Tara gelding quite prominently in the earlier stages but he weakened three furlongs from home. Maybe the good ground wasn't to his liking after all. Perhaps it was too soon, just three days after York.

Racing Post couldn't really be faulted in its report:
Prominent, hard ridden 5f out, weakened 3f out, eased over 1f out

Warwick

A long Summer break was well earned by the hard-working Kayfi so he went back to mum who was obviously glad to see her five-year-old again. On 2 Oct 2007, however, it was back to business when he notched up the fourth visit to Warwick and the fourth time with Steve Drowne riding. This time it was the Class 4 Weatherbys Finance Handicap over two miles with the ground officially Good To Firm. The handicapper had been kind to Kayfi and, based on his last performance, excused him two pounds but, at 9 stone 3 pounds, he was still one of three heaviest of the ten runners. The James Fanshawe-trained Aphorism used his weight advantage of 8-12 to win the contest with Kayfi coming fourth, some sixteen lengths behind the winner. It was a valiant attempt and he did gain 384 pounds! Not weight but money!

Racing Post wasn't too harsh:
Prominent, chased leader 4f out, ridden and edged right over 2f out, weakened over 1f out

Isobel & Ross with Steve Drowne

York

For his next outing, on 13 Oct 2007, a jockey was booked who hadn't ridden him since Windsor, 9 May 2005 - Chris Catlin. This was for the Shepherd Group Stakes Handicap at good 'ole' York, over two-and-quarter miles where the ground was stated as Good To Soft. The handicapper this time had been decidedly kind as he reduced Kayfi's load by five pounds and it showed. He bounded along and was in front on two occasions. Certainly a very determined Kayf Tara gelding. Ultimately, however, he was no match for Missoula but he managed to hold on to second place.

Kayfi at York with Chris Catlin

And our favourite racing journal stated:

Led, jinked right and headed briefly 10f out, soon led again, ridden along and headed 4f out, soon driven and kept on final 2f, no chance with winner

Rather underestimated the effort put in by you-know-who but not a bad review.

Newmarket

Time for a second trip to the home of racing since 1636. Kayfi was booked to ride in the Alfie Westwood Lifetime In Racing Handicap at Newmarket on 2 Nov 2007. The last time he was there just over a year before, he came second to Dr Sharp, only one-and-a-quarter lengths behind. Chris Catlin returned for his third ride in this two-mile contest where the ground was officially Good. Once more it wasn't the ground conditions but the weight. Again he was one of the three heaviest of the ten runners. The winner was Double Banded, five pounds lighter. Kayfi had a bit of a tough time and finished eighth.

Racing Post was once more laconic but fairly accurate:
Chased leaders, ridden over 4f out, weakened over 2f out

York

Although Kayfi was now officially amongst the ranks of the jumping fraternity in the careful hands of a skilled trainer, Isobel decided that there was still a little unfinished business up North on the Flat. So she obviously persuaded Venetia Williams to enter Kayfi in the ripleycollection.com Stakes at York on 15 May 2008. The distance was two-and-a-quarter miles and the ground was Good To Firm. Nothing very promising about that. Old stalwart, Marc Halford, was called up for duty again. There were thirteen contenders. Perhaps Isobel thought this was a good chance for her wonder horse to get his revenge. It was an exciting contest but Kayfi didn't win. He came fourth, BUT he beat his four old rivals – Rose Bien and Numero Due by half a length, Thewhirlingdervish by four-and-three-quarter lengths and Great As Gold by over twenty lengths!!!
That was certainly a memorable day.!

Racing Post certainly put the dampers on it a bit by commenting:
Tracked leaders, headway 4f out, ridden well over 2f out, driven and kept on same pace from over 1f out

York

Sixteen days later we were in York again. The same trainer/jockey team were back on duty in the Coldstream Guards Association Stakes over two-and-a-half miles. The ground was listed as officially Good. A bit déjà vu really. Kayfi came fourth again three-and-a-half lengths behind the unknown horse, Bukit Tinggi, who was ten pounds heavier. BUT three places and nine-and-a-half lengths ahead of Thewhirlingdervish! Revenge again!

Don't you just love **Racing Post**!
Chased leaders, keeping on same pace when slightly hampered over 1f out
RP actually made an excuse for Kayfi! He was 'hampered'

Royal Ascot

One race track we hadn't yet visited which is a favourite of the Queen, was Ascot. Kayfi was scheduled to run there on 21 Jun 2008 and Steve Drowne was booked to be aboard (for the fourth time) in the Queen Alexandra Stakes, two-miles plus and the ground was good to firm. It was perhaps ominous that not one of old buddies ventured to try this one. It was clearly not his race. He came last-but-one. I won't say how many ran!

No arguments with **Racing Post:**

Chased leaders, ridden and losing place when not much room over 3f out, no danger when not much room again over 2f out

Gary, Bill, Isobel, Barbara, Derek, Ross and Sue
at Royal Ascot

York – Winner!

Kayfi now had a well-earned rest in preparation for the jumps season in November which kept him busy until April 2009 with ten races over hurdles. Then on 14 May Isobel couldn't resist the opportunity to let Kayfi defend his crown at York, where he had won theripleycollection.com Stakes the year before. Another pleasant day as regards the weather on the Knavesmire. Everyone seemed to be enjoying themselves. The race, sponsored by the company that produces Horse Racing Colours And Equestrian Jewellery, was a contest over two-and-a-quarter miles with thirteen runners, including our old friend, Rose Bien. Venetia Williams booked Johnny Murtagh to do the steering on ground that was officially listed as Good. I think we were all a little nervous that it was too much to ask for Kayfi to win again. When the race started, we suddenly saw a different Kayfi, already in the lead after four furlongs and going on to be well clear of the field. Johnny Murtagh even had the confidence to ease down in the final furlong as Kayfi was so far ahead! There was talk that Kayfi needed that big win to increase his handicap so that he could run in the Cesarewitch at Newmarket in October!

Racing Post:
Soon with leader, led over 4f out, soon pushed well clear, eased inside final furlong

I think they meant to say that Kayfi **WON by Thirteen lengths,** ahead of Rose Bien!

"A rose by any other name" would still have lost!

Ross with Johnny Murtagh after winning a York

Goodwood

Just six days later we were off for a second time to Goodwood. Kayfi was entered in the Sussex Stayers Stakes over two miles on 20 May. The ground was officially described as Good. Venetia Williams had decided that Jamie Spencer should be on board in this nine-strong field. Kayfi made a courageous attempt to challenge the leader but the pace seemed too fast for him and he was tired about fifty yards from home and quickly lost three places, coming in fifth. Ironically he did one better than the next horse, the Andrew Balding-trained, aptly named, Isabelonabicycle!

Racing Post got it about right
Rousted along from stalls to press leader, ridden over 4f out, upsides under maximum pressure from 3f out, not quicken over 1f out, held when crossed last 50yds and lost 3 places

Royal Ascot

A decision was made to pay another visit to the Queen's local racecourse, just six miles from Windsor Castle. Johnny Murtagh was recalled for duty, presumably in the hope that he could pull off something similar to his thirteen-length victory at York a month earlier. The Ascot Stakes, on 16 June 2009 was a slightly longer contest over almost two-and-a-half miles so that was very welcome. The ground was Good To Firm which was not. It was a large field with twenty runners but none of the old gang were there to take on Kayfi, who, typically raised our hopes when he went into the lead about four furlongs out. He was headed just after that but went into the lead for a second time about two furlongs from home. Unfortunately

he weakened in the final two-hundred yards and slipped back to sixth position.

No complaints about **Racing Post:**
Prominent, led 4f out, soon went right, ridden and headed over 2f out, soon hung left and regained lead, headed over 1f out, weakened final furlong

Isobel, Ross, Barbara, Derek & Gary
at Royal Ascot

Kayfi with Haggis at Royal Ascot

80

Newmarket

After his impressive thirteen-length victory at York, Kayfi's handicap was bumped up to the eighties, which, it was suspected, was the aim of the exercise. So, he was duly qualified to enter the Investec Cesarewitch Trail Handicap at Newmarket on 18 Sep 2010. Since October 2009, Kayfi was officially handled by another trainer, Nigel Twiston-Davies who invited Jim Crowley to do the honours in the two-and-a quarter-mile contest. The ground was good. The 2016 Champion jockey, aboard for the first time, certainly seemed to know how to get the best out of his mount and three furlongs from home, once more, Kayfi seemed to stand every chance. By the two-furlong pole, however, it was déja vu. He weakened very quickly as the fourteen-strong field entered the last furlong and slipped back to ninth.

We could only guess at the reason. The distance was right but the ground was Good. The pace was also fast in the final stages, perhaps too fast for Kayfi.

Racing Post: Chased leaders, ridden 5f out, effort under pressure and every chance 3f out until 2f out, weakened quickly entering final furlong (op 17

Fair comment

Kayfi with Becky at Newmarket

Newmarket

Surprisingly Kayfi gained entry into the Cesarewitch. The contest was set for 16 Oct 2010, once more at Newmarket. This time the going was Good To Soft. No complaints there. Yet another jockey was booked to ride. This time it was David Probert but, whether the partnership didn't work or Kayfi wasn't up to it, he had nothing left three furlongs out and his jockey even eased him down as they entered the last stretch and he finished mid-field, which means that many other horses had a tough race, too.

Racing Post was fair enough: **In touch, headway to chase leaders 10f out, ridden and struggling 6f out, weakened over 3f out, no chance final 2f, eased entering final furlong**

York

Almost a year-and-a-half passed before Kayfi ventured onto the Flat again, during which time the now ten-year-old was kept busy with fifteen National Hunt races. Whether by design or out of pure nostalgia, we found ourselves back at York again on 17 May 2012 for the Investec Specialist Bank Stakes, two-and-a-quarter miles with the going Good. The trainer's son, Willie Twiston-Davies, joined the long-list of jockeys to ride Kayf Aramis. It was good being back on the Knavesmire again after so long but we were not sure what to expect from Kayfi who now spent most of his time mastering the art of getting efficiently over hurdles. To be suddenly confronted with the techniques of racing without obstacles to negotiate after such a long absence, was sure to pose problems. Sure enough, Kayf Aramis' swansong and his forty-second outing on the Flat, turned out to be almost a mirror image of his two previous sorties. He made every effort until about half a mile from home and then weakened and his result in the race appropriately matched his age but, even so, quite a few followed him home.

Let Racing Post have the last word: **Midfield, some headway 7f out, ridden and in touch over 4f out, weakened 3f**

When looking at Kayfi's nine-year career, it's like dealing with two horses – on the one hand the two-mile-plus stayer on the Flat, emulating his champion sire, Kayf Tara, and on the other the indomitable hurdler pitched against some of the best talent in National Hunt racing. The clue to this 'split personality' may lie in the fact that Kayf Tara, since joining the Overbury stud, has become the top British jumps sire, producing champions such as Special Tiara, the Queen Mother Champion Chase victor, and Thistlecrack, winner of the World Hurdle. (More of that in the Jumps section.).

From forty-one Flat races on turf (plus one on the all-weather) Kayfi notched up 4 Wins (3 at York and 1 at Bath), 8 Seconds and 2 Thirds. As they say in the trade, Kayf Aramis doesn't owe anybody anything. He has more than repaid the loyalty and love of his owner/breeder and his hundreds of followers up and down the country. This Aramis is certainly 'One for All'!

There were more exciting times to come but they happened during Kayfi's forty-three outings over hurdles, which you will find in **Jump to it**!

Flat Racing and Jumps Best of Both Worlds
by Barbara Coltman

Kayf Aramis turned out to be a talented all-rounder to the surprise of many, including one trainer who said "he'll never jump."

NEVER SAY NEVER
Kayf Aramis was sent off to do some jump schooling, the trainer declared, after some intensive training "He leaps like a stag"

The Flat Racing season enabled us to enjoy so many summers following him throughout the length and breadth of the country meeting up as a family and enjoying many picnics with the occasional visit to the winner's suite to sip Champagne and get to watch the race again. Nothing quite prepares one for the sheer ecstasy of having your horse win a race. Nothing compares with it. Even a consolation prize of a 2nd, 3rd or even 4th place doesn't figure. After the experience of a win and celebration on the course, the journey home is in a wonderful buoyant mood, reliving every second of the race unlike the times when one's hopes don't materialise and one limps home in silence, waiting for the consoling whisky and an early night!

The majority of racehorse owners wait in hope for that elusive win. I remember a chap in his seventies being interviewed after his horse won. He declared he had waited for over 40 years to experience this moment- and how sweet it was. Isobel's grandmother had an expression, "The stupid have all the luck" Stupid or not, in Isobel's case it was beginner's luck. None of us had any experience in horse racing whatsoever so maybe our expectations were naïve but always positive. We never dwelt on the negative side because we were too ignorant of the sport. When little Kayfi was born, he looked like an origami toy with one ear slightly flapped over. It took a while for him to straighten out, then, as soon as he could run he showed his exuberance around the field. We declared him a future winner – of that there was no doubt!

Jump to It!

Tough stayers who can handle distances of two-and-half to three miles are usually directed towards National Hunt after racing on the Flat for several years. Isobel was obviously thinking ahead. What would Kayfi do in the next two years? He was now a five-year-old and most runners on the Flat have a career span of six to eight years, with notable exceptions. When they reach that age, however, they are inevitably up against the next generation of lively three and four-year-olds. Isobel decided, therefore, to persuade John Spearing to prepare Kayfi for a hurdle race. So between November and January Kayfi had to get used to jumping and on 25 January 2008 a suitable race was found for him, the Emma Lavelle Racing Ltd Maiden Hurdle, over three-and-a-half miles at Newbury. Can't argue about the distance. It certainly wasn't too short. Perhaps a bit over the top, though, for Kayfi's first venture over obstacles. He had a lot to get used to, after all. A 'taller jockey with longer stirrups' (Tony Evans) and the hurdles which had to be taken at speed. At least Kayfi wasn't alone in this ordeal. Of the original twenty runners only twelve finished. The others were all pulled up, including Kayfi after the sixth of twelve hurdles. Some of the runners had given up by the second or third so, taken in context, Kayfi didn't do so badly. Ironically his first race on the Flat wasn't successful, either. After the race, however, things happened. The trainer, John Spearing, said quite bluntly that Kayfi would never make a jumper. Now 'never' is a word that Isobel doesn't readily accept in her vocabulary. You can't 'Dream the impossible dream' with such a word! Within a very short time, (the official notification was on 22 February) Kayfi had left John Spearing's yard and was settled with the successful jumps trainer, Venetia Williams, in Herefordshire.

By the end of March Kayfi was deemed ready for his next National Hunt experience. Sam Thomas was booked to ride him in the two-and-a-half-mile Betfredbingo Maiden Hurdle on soft ground at Wincanton. That combination sounded about right. We were generally not sure what to expect but we trusted that the trainer had got it right. In fact, Kayfi acquitted himself very well under the circumstances. OK, he was at the back of the field for quite some time but he gradually made progress from the seventh hurdle, keeping the leaders well in his sights. Unfortunately his stamina didn't hold out but this was only his second attempt at jumping. The last time at Newbury he was pulled up so he hadn't gone the distance. He stayed on, however, and came third. Third! Even earning £500 prize money!

After 148 days' break with his family in Gloucestershire, Kayfi went back to the Venetia Williams' yard in Aramstone to begin what was to be his most successful season. On 16 November 2008 he was entered for a Class 4 maiden hurdle over two miles, three furlongs at Fontwell. On board was to be Aidan Coleman, who was to experience a highly successful six-ride partnership with Kayf Aramis at the peak of his performance (both horse and jockey!). The result was possibly a hint of better things to come. He came a good Second, just three-and-a-half lengths behind Charlie Mann's Fair Point.

A month later he was back in action at Chepstow (Aidan Coleman. 4/13) and Taunton (Sam Thomas. 2/10).

At the beginning of the New Year Kayfi made the trip to Hereford with Sam Thomas aboard again, finishing 6 out of 12, followed by a trip back to Fontwell for a Novices' hurdle with Liam Treadwell for the first time where he was even the 11/10 favourite. There were three runners and the race looked like it was going to be Kayfi's. He challenged the leader by the eighth hurdle and went into the lead two from home. Unfortunately he made a mistake at the last and was obviously tiring a little. He then appeared not to be comfortable on his own in front and veered to the right on the run-in, perhaps because the paddocks were just opposite and he wanted to go home but he virtually handed victory on a plate to Venetia Williams' other horse, Latanier, with Aidan Coleman aboard in the final fifty yards. Isobel had made the long journey there just with Ross as none of the rest of the family could make it. The disappointment could be heard in her voice during the post-race interview when she even hinted that she 'felt almost like giving up'! Only hinted, mind, because Isobel is definitely a stayer and she was still "dreaming the impossible dream"!

On February 12 there was suddenly a noticeable change in the now seven-year-old Kayf Tara gelding. He seemed to have matured and to be taking on a different attitude to racing. He went back to Chepstow for a third time, having come fourth on the two previous occasions. It was the three-mile Jenkinsons Caterers 1st Choice For Conferences Maiden Hurdle and Aidan Coleman was aboard again. This certainly was a different Kayfi. He was always going well. We were a bit nervous that he took the lead too soon after the third hurdle, knowing his previous habit of wanting to stay close to the other horses. That behaviour now seemed in the past and he went clear to win by a comfortable six lengths. Was this the beginning of the Dream?

Kayfi winner at Chepstow with Venetia Williams, Isobel, Ross and Aidan Coleman

On 20 February Venetia Williams decided on another trip to Warwick, a track that Kayfi seemed to enjoy, having notched up three good Seconds there. Sam Thomas was to do the honours again in this three-mile-one-furlong toteswinger Novices' Hurdle with only four runners. Once more this was not the same horse. He 'made all' as the racing jargon puts it. That is, he went into the lead and stayed there and won the £5000 prize by three-and-a quarter lengths. That made it two wins in a row. Kayfi had never achieved that before.

A month later he was entered for the three-mile Pertemps Final Handicap Hurdle at Cheltenham on Good to Soft ground. So it seemed all to be coming together at last. Kayfi was winning over the longer distances as we always thought he would. But could he win the prestigious prize, thus making it a first-time hat-trick?

The month seemed a long while coming but eventually it was Cheltenham Festival time. Kayfi was due to line up at Prestbury Park on the third day, Thursday 12 March, in the Pertemps Final Handicap Hurdle alongside twenty-one rivals. The distance was three miles and the was officially Good To Soft. It all sounded ideal. Trainer, Venetia Williams, had invited Aidan Coleman for his fourth ride on Kayf Aramis, having ridden him to victory at Chepstow precisely one month earlier. One rival was also aiming for glory and that was Buena Vista ridden by Tom Scudamore. Perhaps more of a threat, however, was the future Grand National winner, Don't Push It, with the then champion jockey, Tony McCoy, aboard. All the Kayfi followers were clearly anxious about how the race would pan out but they kept their thoughts to themselves. Their worries were unnecessary as it turned out. Kayf Aramis was always prominent, taking up the second slot by the fourth hurdle. He was well clear in the lead three furlongs from home and ran on powerfully to beat Buena Vista by two lengths. Needn't have worried about Don't Push It. He didn't and came Seventh!

There was one anxious moment for Aidan Coleman in the last hundred yards. He couldn't see what the racegoers could. As he said afterwards: "I heard something coming in the run-in and I was thinking "not now" because he had been in front for so long. He didn't deserve to get caught but, thank God, it was a loose horse, such a relief." This alarm, in fact, was caused by Heathcliff (Strange how horses lose their name after the jockey comes off!) who had unseated his rider much earlier on but carried on racing, obviously enjoying himself, and passed Kayfi as he neared the post.

Kayfi winning at the Cheltenham Festival with Aidan Coleman

The victory not only marked a unique hat-trick for the seven-year-old Kayfi but also represented a number of first-time achievements. It was owner/breeder Isobel Phipps Coltman's first winner from a first runner at The Festival. It was a first Festival success for jockey Aidan Coleman who had now reached 50 winners that season. For trainer Venetia Williams, it opened her account for that year's Festival and it was her fourth winner in all at this meeting. She had an interesting take on the closing moments of the race: "I think the loose horse helped him a bit in the closing stages, giving him something to run against."

Ireland North and South by Barbara Coltman

Kayf , already having made his name in York and Cheltenham is sent by Twiston-Davies for a jaunt to the Emerald Isle. Isobel, Gary and Ross cross over the Irish Sea to Punchestown where they have the pleasure of meeting up again with an old friend, Nadia Abramowitz and her young daughter, Jessica, who drive down from Bessbrook, thanks to the generosity of farmer John. It's a beautiful day, the children have fun chasing each other around and Nadia and Isobel leaving them to it as they catch up on years of news and shared experiences of being 'Mums', since the last time they met was as schoolgirls on blissful family holidays on the West Coast of Ireland, shared with four rowdy and resourceful brothers The house we stayed in was right on the beautiful beach where the children enjoyed donkey rides whose telephone number was 'Inch 11'

This being Ireland the race track was pure emerald green and Kayfi in his green colours looked very much at home under the whip of Richard Johnson. They set off at a great pace ahead of the pack looking good and clearly enjoying the occasion, Enough said. Clearly he wasn't going to pay his way that day!.

Several years on I was visiting Nadia on her home territory in Armagh. We caught the local bus to go to Newry and we were reminiscing about Kayfi's race at Punchestown when suddenly the bus juddered to an emergency stop. The bus driver

Nadia, Isobel, Jessica and Ross

leans out from his seat and asks us if he's heard right and we were talking about Kayf Aramis. Yes, Isobel nodded. ' Ah, begorrah' exclaimed the bus driver. "I know dat hoss. I put money on him Won Big!"

So, what's in a name? **MAGIC!**

That wasn't the only occasion his name was fondly recalled. All around the country, whether hard-bitten, betting people, who daily follow racing or occasional race goers who remembered their day at Cheltenham on March 12th. 2009. People seem to remember the diminutive Kayf Aramis, the really genuine racing hero.

Kayf Aramis appeared thirty-three more times on the track after his triumph at Cheltenham on 12 March 2009, winning on the Flat at York two months later.

Reunited with **Becky** at the yard of Nigel Twiston-Davies, Kayfi moved up to Graded company. Becky enjoyed a wonderful partnership with Kayfi, spanning nine years, having looked after him on the Flat.

Kayfi produced some excellent Places at a number of top racecourses including three Seconds and two Thirds at Cheltenham; a Second and Third in the **Grade 2 Rendlesham at Haydock**; Second in the **Grade 2 West Yorkshire Hurdle at Wetherby**, and two Fourths in the **Grade 1 Long Walk Hurdle at Newbury**.

Becky with Kayfi at Nigel Twiston-Davies yard

2nd in Grade 2 Rendlesham at Haydock
with Paddy Brennan and Becky

2nd in Grade 2 West Yorkshire Hurdle at Wetherby
with Paddy Brennan

3rd Grade 2 Rendlesham at Haydock
with San Twiston-Davies

Overall Kayf Aramis lined up in 43 races, won 3 of them, produced eight Seconds and five Thirds. That compares with his record on the Flat where he ran 41 (plus one on the all-weather) in total, winning 4, runner-up 8 times and Second twice.

Kayf Aramis' final race was at Ffos Las on 6 May 2013. He then retired at the young age of eleven which can be calculated as the equivalent of thirty-three in human terms.

Kayfi

Part 3 How It All Began

MISTY

Isobel and Misty

The story of a pony that morphed into a race horse

Misty, the beautiful half Arab, half Welsh pony who for five years trotted forth from the back garden in Golders Green NW11, finally breathed her last in a Gloucestershire field on Midsummer's Day June 21 2000. She was buried the following day in the shade of an old crab apple tree under which she had fallen, an idyllic spot with a view to one of the famous Gloucestershire hills topped with a corona of trees. She was an exquisite creature with huge appealing eyes fringed by long white eye lashes. There was a certain Moorish hauteur about her and a quick intelligence that at times could be interpreted as mischief. For the five years she was in the area she attracted a huge fan club. Isobel, then fourteen and a pupil at Henrietta Barnett School, was frequently seen on the Suburb roads and, with special permission from the GLC, along certain tracks all over Hampstead Heath. Misty's early life was researched and we found that she had been a good jumper and had originally hailed from Great Dunmow in Essex. We visited one of her past owners in Hertfordshire, a Lennie Hawkins, whose daughter won many rosettes competing on Misty. These trophies were proudly displayed around the walls of their sitting room.

95

Isobel first came across Misty at College Farm, a tract of green land and old farm buildings in Barnet, along the busy Regent's Park Road, where even today one can see sheep, horses or cattle grazing in their unlikely location, attracting the young and old to pause and 'stare as long as sheep or cows.' A piece of history magically kept from the clutches of developers. In return for mucking out after school and at weekends, Isobel was allowed the occasional ride and later on even to compete in the small gymkhanas that were held from time to time. On those occasion I remember that Misty's former jumping prowess strangely eluded her, much to the chagrin of her keen and competitive rider.

This was the start of Isobel's passion for horses, though evidence of her love for animals, especially horses, was clear from her infant and junior school art. Neat little cats, rough collies (how prophetic as later she would care for a rescued cat called Broby and two rescued rough collies named Shady and Ricky) and most of all, rows and rows of neatly-hooved ponies. These were drawn, coloured and painted at every opportunity in every notebook and on every cover.

What started her off on the 'ruinous road to racing' was an innocent enough donkey ride up by the Whitestone Pond in Hampstead. A few donkeys, well past their seaside galloping days, were led around the back towards Admiral's House before returning over the Heath back to the pond where they rested in the shade of the tree till the next batch of eager children disrupted their daydreams. The donkey rides made way for pony riding in Epping Forest where there was no doubt that Isobel had 'discovered her seat.'

Isobel riding in Epping Forest with Derek

Isobel on Rusty on the Heath

Her confidence grew as she joined rides, led by Jill, a character not unlike one from Thelwell's novels, who would lead her little charges from the stables in Strawberry Vale over the main North End Road onto the Heath Extension. Isobel's favourite pony was called Rusty, a willing creature whose colour reflected his name, though sometimes she was given an old nag to ride, possibly as she was the only one not to complain when she was shouted at for not keeping up with the group as the wayward pony listened not to the rider but its tum and stopped at every verge to eat grass. After one such event I found Isobel weeping in her bedroom nursing her hands cut through by the reins, yet blaming only herself for not managing her mount better. Later, in the sixth form, she volunteered to work at City Farm for her work experience, which proved to be both an exhilarating and a healthy option instead of working in offices or shops. Part of her duties was to exercise the horses and later on she took lessons from a very talented young girl called Mary Wanless who wrote 'Riding with the Mind.'

City Farm, which was set up in 1972 on a piece of derelict land in Kentish Town, is to celebrate its fortieth anniversary in 2012. The idea of introducing children living in overcrowded Inner London areas to country life on their doorstep was the inspiration of a young American, Ed Berman, who cajoled British Rail to allow him to use a piece of their land for the benefit of the local community. The story we heard at the time was that Ed Berman was diagnosed with cancer and, believing he might not live to a ripe old age, threw himself into projects for the benefit of local people. He set up The Almost Free Theatre, with the young Simon Callow and Anthony Sher, rehearsing to the cacophony of a growing number of farmyard animals in the background.

Local children were encouraged to take responsibility for looking after the animals helping to help feed, muck out and learn about animal husbandry.

This model proved so successful that it has spawned many city farms all round London. For this work he was given an honour by the Queen.

What is more, I gather he is still very much alive continuing his public spirited work.

Isobel's life, from then on, centred around the equine scene. Pony Club news and magazines were devoured. She entered and won competitions, kitting herself out practically from head to foot in riding gear and equipment including a copy of Ryan's Son's saddle donated by the champion rider, John Whittaker which Isobel won in a competition, helped by her father.

Riding holidays followed in Wales with challenging mounts to conquer and Gypsy, a retired blind pit pony, to befriend. And what had previously been restful holidays in the South of France turned out to be riding adventures in the Camargue with her brothers given scary mounts to ride named Ouragan and Volcane who took off, with their young charges yelling, 'arrête, arrête' to no avail whilst their little sister rode with great mastery, controlling her mount perfectly.

FROM COLLEGE FARM TO GOLDERS GREEN

The mutually convenient arrangement with Misty's owner, Clare, came to an end when, as often happens at that age, boyfriends take precedence over horses and so Misty was sold on. Deprived of her beloved Misty, Isobel was much distraught and when, a few weeks later, she discovered that Misty was being kept in some stables North of London. She begged me to drive up there. It seemed an innocent enough request. Little did I know what that the visit would lead to.

The sight that met our eyes was truly pitiful. Here was this exquisite creature shut in her box looking seriously depressed. She was neither being fed well nor exercised. Her hooves had grown to such an extent that further delay in calling the blacksmith would have caused permanent damage to her legs. We arranged for Misty to be given extra food and to be re-shod so that on out next visit we were able to walk her out. On her first outing Misty was like a condemned man having been granted his freedom. It was a breezy day when we walked her up the lane. The wind blew her mane as she walked elegantly beside Isobel, occasionally stopping to look over the hedge at the grazing sheep with huge bewilderment in her eyes. That day as I was leaving I whispered in Misty's ear.

"We'll do whatever we can to get you out of here, you beauty."

My vow preceded Isobel's pleas on the journey home to buy Misty and rescue her from her uncaring owner. Knowing the expense of keeping a horse in stables in London, my mind went to overdrive in lateral thinking. I remembered Frances Whitfield, telling me that as a child she kept her pony in a garage in Reading on the London Road and I also remembered that years ago a circus performer kept his horse in the basement of his house in Finchley Road leading him up and down the steep stone steps. Then I thought about and discounted the idea of keeping a pony in the front room as did a young woman in the West Country. I decided the best solution would be for Misty to be kept in our extended garden which we acquired with our semi-detached house. There was only one big problem. The side of the house was too narrow to bring a pony through to the front and the back had no access as the garden backed onto the car park of the then YHA which was run by Brian Rance, a countryman at heart. That was the obvious solution as the YHA was on Wellgarth Rd which led directly to the Heath Extension with its convenient horse track. So Brian was approached and, after checking with his Head Office, he happily accepted the plan that would allow us to put a gate in our fence to allow Misty an exit. The council had to admit that since the time that horses were kept in mews there was no legislations preventing us from keeping the horse in our back garden and finally, when all the plans had been laid, Derek, my husband, capitulated when the neighbours began asking him in the street, "So, when is the horse coming?"

For a man who had never built anything more than a stool in his woodwork class, Derek threw himself into the construction of a stable from the shell of an old summer house of which only the solid brick back wall and low side walls remained. It was just before Christmas and the weather was not always benign and there was the added problem of cutting down one of the sycamore trees that had grown inside the carcass of the building overtime. First of all he constructed the stable door which worked out exceedingly well, very solid and then proceeded to make the walls out of fencing panels the whole being held together with a great deal of nails. It was a bigger undertaking than he had first thought and he took ten days off work and worked practically round the clock to construct his stable. First the walls, then the roof was fixed, not an easy matter as he had to fit the

Misty's stable in Summer

roof around the big trunk of the remaining sycamore and finally the door was fitted. No mean feat for a beginner and the incessant sound of the hammer and saw were heard throughout the Christmas season. Inside the stable the old water tank was emptied of its mud and cleaned up for horse food storage and shelves were fitted for straw and hay and finally hooks for the saddle and reins. Electric wiring was trailed along the fence from the house and under the bottom garden to provide light. A short track led to the newly constructed gate in the back fence and Misty even had a small yard outside her stable for her to take the air. She was hemmed in by a thin pole, yet for all her strength she never broke through it to the tasty grass beyond which served as our lawn. On pleasant, sunny days when we were out in the garden she was allowed out to join us and keep the grass down so there was no need of a lawnmower.

The day had arrived for Misty to try out her new home. It was January 1st, 1983, a bitterly cold day with a nasty drizzle in the air. Isobel rode Misty down from Hertfordshire along the busy main roads with Derek accompanying her in the car until she got to Finchley and knew her way home. By the time the pony and rider arrived at the stable it was already beginning to get dark. The stable was lit warmly and a wonderful smell of fresh straw emanated from it. Some warm mash was awaiting the weary traveller and sweet tasting hay was in the net. A supply of water and blankets for warmth stood by. The scene could not have been more inviting, however Misty refused point

Misty's stable in Winter

blank to enter her new abode and no amount of cajoling or pushing could make her budge. She stood stubbornly outside in the rain whilst Isobel moved inside the stable trying to warm up with hot cup-a-soups. She would not abandon her charge and, just as we thought we would have to keep vigil overnight, Misty took one step forward, two steps back and suddenly lunged at the entrance and made for the food. Misty was safe at last.

From then on Misty and her young rider became a familiar and welcome sight around the neighbourhood. Isobel ventured further afield as she and Misty grew more confident in negotiating the busy road junctions and even appeared outside her grandmother's house in Muswell Hill.

A Christmas treat for Misty

Every Wednesday, instead of going to games, Isobel would cut school and ride Misty around the Heath. One day just as she was on the track closest to Hampstead lane, a car stopped, the window was wound down and, much to Isobel's horror, Miss Marjoribanks, her formidable headmistress, leant her head out and watched for a while, then gestured with her hand, wound the window up and continued on her way back to the Henrietta Barnett School in Central Square in Hampstead Garden Suburb, no doubt reflecting on the fact that she too had skipped school perhaps on one of her long lunches that she used to enjoy. Isobel continued to ride Misty on Wednesday afternoons and nothing was ever said about her exploits. Neighbours were delighted to have a horse in their midst. Old Mr Wickert pressed £10 into Isobel's hand for extra hay and Erica was glad of the manure for her roses. In fact everybody's roses in the road did well over that period. Derek then logically thought that instead of taking loads of manure to the dump, the local gardeners at the allotments would be glad of it, so he put a message up on the gate, but alas, there were no takers, so he continued his weekly trip with black bins filled with used straw and manure to the tip. On one occasion as he was unloading his cargo, one of the bags split open the contents pouring out onto the shoe of the man in charge. 'SH**!' he shouted, to which Derek answered, 'Yes, that's right!'

In summer, when the ground was firm, Misty was often allowed to roam freely around the back extension and mingle with family and guests. The photograph of Misty overlooking two chess players, Dominic and Lawrence, is much valued. 'Queen to Knight two' she seems to advise with a turn of her head. She did no damage to the

Lawrence and Dominic playing chess

vegetable beds or the fruit trees, unlike one visitor, Daisy the goat, who came with Brian Rance to a Sunday tea party. Daisy was no shrinking violet, she immediately took over the whole garden seeing it her right to gobble up any vegetation she came across and the lettuces and carrot and beetroot tops were more to her liking than grass. She was immensely strong and none of us could hold her back. Needless to say, Daisy did not visit again!

At first we had an old Irish blacksmith to shoe her. He used to arrive with his old van, park outside our gate in the car park of the YHA, stoke up a fire, trim Misty's feet, cut off a length of metal strip and fashion it to fit exactly. Bespoke shoes, so to speak. Each time he came he attracted a crowd of back packers watching his skill in such an unusual venue.

The old farrier was followed by Mr Tonks and Ginger, both from the St John's Wood Barracks, who were possibly 'supplementing' their Army pay. The process was much more streamlined

Misty gets her toe nail beauty treatment

with cold shoeing. There was no stoking of fire and the ready made shoes just needed minor alterations. Some of the charm of the traditional blacksmith had gone. Not every shoeing went according to plan. I remember one occasion when Isobel had tethered Misty to the back fence and Ginger was about to fit a shoe, a bird fluttered down from the tree and Misty took fright and took off, demolishing most of the back fence and dragging it with her. In those days Derek used to cycle to the IOD and that day he came home to find not only the back gate missing but the whole back fence.

There was always the nagging thought that Misty might have to be passed on, so Isobel made sure that wouldn't happen through an unfortunate accident that gave her the means to keep her pony forever. One day, when cycling to school in the Suburb, she was knocked down by a taxi, which turned left when Isobel had right of way. The case went to court and Isobel was awarded the exact sum of money Derek had paid for Misty. She insisted that her father took the money so she became the legal owner, except of course the maintenance costs, which still remained Derek's responsibility!

YORK

Time had come for Isobel to go to University. To Derek, whose fetching supplies and carting away waste was essential to the arrangement, it became clear that when Isobel went up to York, Misty would have to go too. I had played my part in bringing Misty to Golders Green, now it was up to father and daughter to make the arrangements for Misty to go to university. Several stables were visited before one in Naburn was found to be acceptable. One farmer, on being asked whether she could do dressage, looked rather puzzled, then, after a long pause, taking his pipe out of his mouth mumbled, "Ee, it's like wat-ching p-aint dry'!

Naturally Isobel's priorities at York were riding Misty and going to the races. Little did she know then that in years to come, the racing horse she bred, Kayf Aramis, would win three times in the May Festival. They were sweet, sweet victories, but that is another story. Isobel joined the University Riding Club and delighted her fellow students by riding Misty around the campus. Despite the time spent on horses not only did Isobel get a decent degree in Linguistics but also found time to play cello with the university orchestra in a stirring performance of Beethoven's Requiem at the beautiful York Minster.

LONDON in the HOLIDAYS

Back in London there were forays to Rotten Row and horse shows. One in Kensington Gardens proved memorable for Misty refusing to jump. A great many hours had gone into turning her out beautifully for the show, brushing her coat, combing the mane and putting oil on the hooves so she would not be out of place with the smart set on their immaculate horses. Luckily Misty's honour was saved to a certain degree by the fact that some of the ultra-smart horses also refused at the first fence.

Locally there will be those who remember a saddled, riderless pony galloping furiously through the Suburb, over the busy North Circular (The lights must have been with her) to return to her former stables at College Farm in Regent's Park Road. It was on an afternoon when Isobel had gone to Stratford on Avon with the school and I decided to take Misty out on the Heath Extension for her customary afternoon ride. We started off pleasantly enough with a gentle walk along the top of the track but alas, I was not to know that at the corner she was used to taking off at a gallop. Not being a strong rider I panicked, my riding hat falling over my eyes and, unable to pull her up, instinctively I grabbed hold of her neck. The next thing I knew I was waking up in the Royal Free Hospital with a policeman leaning over me saying, 'Don't worry madam, your horse is safe.' I asked 'What horse? Apparently I was dragged along the track, my sweater getting crammed full of dead leaves, which were then copiously scattered throughout the hospital corridors. Years later when I had the misfortune of landing up at the Royal Free again, that incident was recalled by some of the nurses.

On another occasion Isobel was riding out in the snow when Misty slipped on some ice and unseated her rider. On this occasion Misty stayed with her injured owner. Luckily a young man happened to be driving by who was familiar with spooked horses and first he calmed and secured Misty and then took care of Isobel. On such occasions when Isobel was unable to ride Misty and I was unwilling to, after my incident, Derek took over by taking the reins and pulling Misty behind him at a jog much to the amusement of dog walkers.

POST UNIVERSITY

Although Isobel and Misty were inseparable, we detected a certain amount of pragmatism creeping in when it suited. For instance, when she was in Toulouse for the year, Amy Klein was entrusted with looking after Misty, which she did with great pleasure and competence. Similar arrangements were made to allow Isobel to spend time in Barcelona and later in Jerez as well as the six months she spent in Chicago. All these trips involved horses in some way. Although she went out to teach English in Barcelona, she soon found a riding establishment where she spent many enjoyable hours. One day we got a call from Isobel saying that a Japanese Olympic rider had offered to give her his horse. It sounded an offer too good to be true and therefore one to be resisted especially when I asked Isobel how would she get the animal back to the UK. 'Oh, ride him back' she replied. Luckily she was persuaded on that occasion not to follow her mad plan. It turned out that the kind Japanese wanted to make sure his horse would be well looked after as the animal was retiring from sport and who else but a decent English girl could be trusted to look after the horse he loved and had competed on for years.

When EU money was being thrown at Spain many schemes were set up to enrich the young entrepreneurs who took up the challenge. One day I saw an advertisement in The Guardian giving scholarships to youngsters who wanted work experience in Spain. Isobel applied to the Domecq Establishment in Jerez to learn to ride and perform on their beautiful white steeds. She arrived to find that it was a male-only preserve and her job would be to muck out the stables. She was incensed and marched into Don Domecq's office and demanded to be given the opportunities she had come for. He crumbled in front of the strength of argument of this English girl and Isobel was given every encouragement to learn the craft. Curiously from the time she arrived in Jerez to the time she left she noticed that the two young men who had set this up were gradually changing from relative paupers to wealthy looking young-men- about- town driving sports cars. EU money well spent then! One can only surmise how they built on their success to gain employment in the corridors of power at the EU Headquarters in Brussels.

Teaching riding at an establishment in the smart suburbs of Chicago for six months Isobel witnessed the roughness and sometimes cruelty of the Mexican hands. Before coming home I joined her on an adventure going from Chicago to Denver by train then driving across the Rockies and plains to the West Coast. Wherever there were horses to be ridden Isobel would take the opportunity to mount and explore the countryside. One memorable ride was at the stunning Bryce Canyon where the cowboy, who led the ride, asked Isobel if she would go to the movies with him, till he noticed her chaperone. As the movies were a cool 65 miles away it didn't seem practical!

Another time whilst we were driving off track trying to find a dude ranch, we came across an old cowboy who took her for a half day ride up into the hills to an ancient sacred Indian eagle hunting ground. There she learnt much of the Indian ways and customs, in fact she got quite adept at doing the rain dance and chant.

NEW ADVENTURE BEGINS IN HEREFORDSHIRE ENDING IN GLOUCESTERSHIRE

However all good things come to an end and Isobel returned home to begin work at the Institute of Linguists where her young boss turned out to love horses and music so the pair got on very well. It was also time for Misty to move on out of the garden to a field in Mill Hill where she would join the second member of Isobel's horse family, a fine young chestnut thoroughbred mare, named Ara, which Isobel bought without our knowledge but with the financial help and connivance of her grandfather.

Isobel and Ara 1Isob

106

The horses remained in the field over several years until finally Isobel gave up her job with the IOL and moved lock stock and two horses out to Herefordshire where, she hoped, a bright future would await her in riding and competing with another horse-mad woman. The small farm was in beautiful countryside but the shortcoming was quickly made clear when bailiffs started banging on the door and, despite trying to find work in Hereford, there was none available. Before the inevitable happened, Isobel moved out, totally unsure where to go. London was not an option as she decided to make her life in the country permanent. Her first priority was to house the horses, which she did, in stables near Hartpury. Then she found accommodation in a large, shared country house and proceeded to look for work. Sharing the house was a young local man, Gary, who took over the reins, so to speak, and helped to rehouse the horses and generally was a helpful and dependable shoulder to rest on. So much so that on September 12 1998 they were married in the historic Ashleworth church of St Andrew and Bartholomew, whose roots go back to the Saxon times and where generations of Gary's family have celebrated important occasions. Both Misty and Ara, groomed beautifully for the special day and bedecked with old brasses kindly lent by someone in the village, greeting the bride and groom. The reception was at Corse Lawn Hotel for family and friends and in the evening Gary's parents hosted a jolly reception for the whole village at their daughter and son-in-law's fishing inn, The Watersmeet.

The couple moved into a little house with their two rescued rough haired collies, Ricky and Shady and Broby the cat who had missed Isobel greatly when she moved from Hereford. One day, when Isobel returned to pick up her mail, the kitten, whose foot had been crushed by one of the horses followed her before jumping over the tall grass. He was emaciated and sick with cat 'flu' so Isobel had no hesitation in taking him with her leaving a note for the owner.

The horses were housed with Paul, on whose lovely farm where they frolicked in the sun in the old apple orchard with a view towards one of the lovely Gloucestershire hills, with what appears to be a coronet on its summit. The coronet is of the 50 trees planted to commemorate the Golden Jubilee of Queen Victoria's reign. It was there that one calm, sunny late afternoon, on Mid-Summer's Day, 21 June 2000, when Isobel came to feed them, that she turned to find Misty had died suddenly from an aneurism, falling where, just minutes before, she had been contentedly eating grass. Young Tom rushed to pick flowers from the garden when he heard the sad news, it was with such affection Misty was regarded by everyone who knew her. She was buried gently the following day in the shade of the old crab apple tree under which she had fallen, her grave covered with May blossom and roses.

Misty has been much missed, after all, she had been Isobel's companion for over seventeen years and she is irreplaceable. By taking responsibility for Misty from an early age, Isobel acquired a lot of confidence, poise and strength and it also has to be said that Misty was exceptionally lucky to have had such a caring mistress. The two of them are commemorated on a bollard in Hyde Park. The bollards were erected to celebrate the 1690-1990 Tercentenary celebration of Rotten Row. Misty's bollard stands roughly opposite Rutland Gate.

Barbara Coltman March 2010

Appendix Kayf Aramis Race Record

KAYF ARAMIS

After 85 starts, (41 on the flat, 43 over hurdles and 1 all-weather), totalling 7 wins (4 on the flat and 3 over jumps), 16 seconds, 7 thirds and 8 fourths, with earnings of £153,670, **KAYF ARAMIS** bowed out of the competitive racing world on 6th May 2013. He was born on 27th April, 2002, appropriately in the Chinese Year of the Horse and his illustrious Sire is Kayf Tara, the champion two-miler stayer, winner of the Ascot Gold Cup (twice) the Irish St. Leger (twice), the Yorkshire Cup and the Goodwood Cup.

Kayf Aramis's racing career began on 12th June 2004 at Sandown in the *Palletline plc Maiden Stakes* and ended on 6th May 2013 at Ffos Las in the *Parker Plant Eisteddfod Handicap Hurdle*. In those nine years he raced at 26 tracks from Aintree to Ascot, Wetherby to Warwick. His memorable successes, however, were at Cheltenham, where he appeared on **17** occasions and won the *Pertemps Final (Handicap Hurdle)*in 2009 and on the flat at York (9 outings) where he won the *Sportsman Racing Stakes (Handicap)*in 2006, the Robert *Pratt Memorial Stakes (Handicap)*in 2007 and*theripleycollection.com Stakes (Handicap)*in 2009, having failed to make it a hat-trick in 2008. Equally impressive was his 2nd in *The Rendlesham Hurdle Grade 2*in February 2010, followed by a similar success in *The West Yorkshire Hurdle Race Grade 2* at Wetherby in October of the same year.

A total of 25 jockeys have had the pleasure of riding the 'diminutive' Kayf Aramis, as some racing commentators good-naturedly called him; 14 of them only once each. Paddy Brennan had the most rides with 14, 13 over hurdles and one on the flat in a special race at Goodwood for National Hunt jockeys, producing three 2nds, two 3rds and two 4ths. Sam Twiston-Davies also rode 13 times over jumps and notched up two 2nds and one 3rd. On the flat, Paul Quinn (8 rides, two 1sts and one 2nd), who rode him for the year 2005–2006, produced Kayf Aramis's first-ever win at Bath and his first win (of the eventual three) at York.

To Aidan Coleman, however, who was aboard for a total of seven rides (two 1sts, two 2nds and one 4th), from November 2008 to April 2009, goes the honour of helping the son of Kayf Tara to his first win over hurdles at Chepstow in February 2009 and the crowning glory of being victorious in the Cheltenham *Pertemps Final (Handicap Hurdle)*, exactly one month later. Kayf Aramis's other wins were with Marc Halford (11 rides, 2006-2008 - one 1st, four 2nds, one 3rd and three 4ths.) and Sam Thomas (4 rides 2008-2009, one 1st, one 2nd and one 3rd).

One of the outstanding races on the flat was undoubtedly in partnership with Johnny Murtagh (2 rides May and June 2009), when Kayf Aramis, on his final appearance at York in May 2009, won *theripleycollection.com Stakes (Handicap)* by 13 lengths.

Not a bad career for this champion, written off by one trainer as not capable of becoming a jumper and by a well-known jockey on the flat as 'not having any class'!

Overbury Stud: *"Kayf Tara's ultra-tough dual-purpose son Kayf Aramis□"*

Aidan Coleman□□□□: *"Old favourite of mine Kayf Aramis, who gave me my first ever winner at the Cheltenham Festival...He battles so hard."*

Aramis Day at the Races

Three Aramis horses raced on Saturday 4th February 2013 and all were successful

KAYF ARAMIS 3RD AT WETHERBY!

KAYF ARAMIS led the field a merry dance, enjoying himself up front and leaving the others struggling in his wake. He was still leading 2 out when he hit the hurdle and stumbled on landing – something he has never done in all his 40 races over hurdles. Well done to jockey Dave Crosse for sticking on and getting him to 3rd place and very nearly a win.

Kayfi with Dave Crosse and Becky

ZAYFIRE ARAMIS 3RD IN HIS FIRST-EVER RACE!
(Nephew of Kayfi)

Next it was the turn of **ZAYFIRE ARAMIS** in a bumper. He showed plenty of family spirit and got into the lead at 3 out. Then perhaps his inexperience told in the final stages but he held on gamely for a well-earned 3rd. His race was also not without incident with Dave Crosse being unseated on the way to post! Apparently, he went down with another rider for company, and as they got down to the start, Dave told the other jockey he was okay now. Zayfire promptly jinked at a hurdle and put Dave on the floor! Luckily Zayfire didn't go far and was soon caught.

KAYLIF ARAMIS WINS AT FFOS LAS!
(Full brother to Kayfi)

To cap a brilliant day at the races, **KAYLIF ARAMIS**, Kayf's full brother won at Ffos Las for Nigel Twiston-Davies. With Sam Twiston-Davies on board they beat Tony McCoy on The Bear Trap by a head.

This was the most successful days for the ARAMIS stud. Larger stud farms and wealthy horse owners may think nothing of entering more than one horse in races on the same day but we bred these three horses, KAYF ARAMIS, KAYLIF ARAMIS and ZAYFIRE ARAMIS in muddy, rented fields and they are all in training with Nigel Twiston-Davies. All three of them raced on Saturday and produced a Winner and two 3rds. That's a great story!

A good day for the Aramis clan! **All for One, One for All!**

Zayfi, Kaylif and Kayfi at home

Kayf Aramis Race Record

	RUNS	1sts	2nds	3rds	WINNINGS	EARNINGS
JUMP	43	3	8	5	£53,251	£109,099
FLAT	42	4	8	2	£25,583	£44,571
TOTAL	85	7	16	7	£78,835	£153,670

Kayf Aramis Racecourse Appearances

TRACK	RACED	JUMPS	FLAT	1sts	2nds	3rds	4ths
CHELTENHAM	17	17	0	1	3	2	0
YORK	9	0	9	3	1		2
PONTEFRACT	7	0	7		2	1	0
NEWBURY	6	5	1				2
WARWICK	6	1	5	1	3		
HAYDOCK	5	5	0		1	1	
NEWMARKET	4	0	4		1		
GOODWOOD	4	0	4		1		
ASCOT	3	2	1				
CHEPSTOW	3	2	1	1			2
WETHERBY	2	2	0		1	1	
BATH	2	0	2	1			
BEVERLEY	2	0	2			1	1
FONTWELL	2	2	0		2		
AINTREE	2	2	0				
TAUNTON	1	1	0		1		
WINCANTON	1	1	0			1	
NOTTINGHAM	1	0	1				1

Kayf Aramis also raced once at each of the following tracks: **Windsor, Hereford, Newcastle, Ffos Las, Exeter, Punchestown, Sandown, Kempton**

Kayf Aramis Jockeys

JOCKEY	Rides	1st	2nd	3rd	4th
Paddy Brennan	14		3	2	2
Sam Twiston-Davies	13		2	1	
Marc Halford	11	1	4	1	3
Paul Quinn	8	2	1		
Aidan Coleman	7	2	2		1
Steve Drowne	5		1		1
Sam Thomas	4	1	1	1	
Chris Catlin	3		1		
Sam Hitchcott	2			1	1
Dave Crosse	2			1	
Johnny Murtagh	2	1			
David England	1				
William Twiston-Davies	1				
David Probert	1				
Jim Crowley	1				
Richard Johnson	1				
Jamie Spencer	1				
Liam Treadwell	1		1		
Tony Evans	1				
Jimmy Quinn	1				
Kerrin McEvoy	1				
Frankie McDonald	1				
Neil Chalmers	1				1
Steve Carson	1				
Lee Enstone	1				

Printed in Great Britain
by Amazon

10994397R00066